# Cambridge IGCSE®
# First Language English
## Teacher's Resource

CAMBRIDGE UNIVERSITY PRESS
Cambridge, New York, Melbourne, Madrid, Cape Town,
Singapore, São Paulo, Delhi, Mexico City

Cambridge University Press
The Edinburgh Building, Cambridge CB2 8RU, UK

www.cambridge.org
Information on this title: www.cambridge.org/9780521743693

© Cambridge University Press 2010

This publication is in copyright. Subject to statutory exception
and to the provisions of relevant collective licensing agreements,
no reproduction of any part may take place without the written
permission of Cambridge University Press.

First published 2010
3rd printing 2012

Printed in the United Kingdom at the University Press, Cambridge

*A catalogue record for this publication is available from the British Library*

ISBN 978-0-521-74369-3 Paperback with CD-ROM

Cover image: © Nick Servian / Alamy

Every effort has been made to reach copyright holders of material in this book
previously published elsewhere. The publisher would be pleased to hear from
anyone whose rights they have unwittingly infringed.

Cambridge University Press has no responsibility for the persistence or
accuracy of URLs for external or third-party internet websites referred to in
this publication, and does not guarantee that any content on such websites is,
or will remain, accurate or appropriate. Information regarding prices, travel
timetables and other factual information given in this work is correct at
the time of first printing but Cambridge University Press does not guarantee
the accuracy of such information thereafter.

® IGCSE is the registered trademark of University of Cambridge International Examinations

NOTICE TO TEACHERS
The photocopy masters in this publication may be photocopied or distributed
free of charge for classroom use within the school or institution which
purchases the publication. Worksheets and copies of them remain in the
copyright of Cambridge University Press and such copies may not be
distributed or used in any way outside the purchasing institution.

# Contents

Introduction   v
*About the Teacher's Resource*   v
*Using the resource*   vi
*Notes*   vii

Skills and tasks grid   viii

## Part 1   Responding to reading   1
Unit 1   Taking a break   1
Unit 2   The falling wall   6
Unit 3   The gentle touch   9
Unit 4   City portraits   17

## Part 2   Stylistic effects   24
Unit 5   Memorable characters   24
Unit 6   Just walking   29
Unit 7   Dislocation   35
Unit 8   Revisiting   42

## Part 3   Summary   45
Unit 9   Missing persons   45
Unit 10   Pretend friends   51
Unit 11   Sharks and crocs!   58
Unit 12   Caught in the web   67

## Part 4   Directed writing   73
Unit 13   Kept apart   73
Unit 14   Native speakers   80
Unit 15   Dedicated and determined   85
Unit 16   To board or not to board   89

## Part 5     Composition                                                              96

### Argument                                                                            96
Unit 17     Fur and against                                                             96

Unit 18     Google generation                                                          103

### Description                                                                        111
Unit 19     Prized possession                                                          111

Unit 20     Building dreams                                                            115

### Narrative                                                                          120
Unit 21     Crucial decisions                                                          120

Unit 22     Fables, tales and sagas                                                    126

## Part 6     Coursework                                                              134

### Informative/discursive                                                             134
Unit 23     Daily lives                                                                134

Unit 24     Hyper-reality                                                              144

### Descriptive/narrative                                                              148
Unit 25     Seeing the future                                                          148

Unit 26     Famous face                                                                152

### Evaluation of argument                                                             155
Unit 27     Self-esteem v. self-control                                                155

Unit 28     Science or sentiment?                                                      160

Acknowledgements                                                                       166

# Introduction

## About the *Teacher's Resource*

This *Teacher's Resource* has been produced to support teachers overseas and in the UK with the delivery of CIE 0500 (and 0522 Cambridge International Certficate) First Language English syllabus. It is suitable for all combinations and options, whichever have been selected by the centre (Reading Paper 1 or 2 plus Writing Paper 3 or 4), including the optional Paper 5 or Paper 6 Speaking and Listening component. It attempts to cover everything which is relevant – skills, materials, resources, approaches, tasks, advice – to the delivery of the English Language curriculum at this level.

The resource is part of the Cambridge IGCSE First Language English suite by the same author, consisting of a coursebook and a student workbook (both third edition 2010). The resource also complements the existing resources and training available from CIE: teacher and student support websites, scheme of work, past papers, mark schemes, examiner reports, model answers, teacher discussion forum, face-to-face training sessions, and self-study or tutored online professional development courses.

The *Teacher's Resource* was conceived as a response to the needs of teachers and students preparing for the IGCSE First Language English exam and to the difficulties in some parts of the world of acquiring suitable resources or having access to training opportunities. Specifically designed for the busy, inexperienced or resource-challenged teacher, this publication is unique in that it contains *in one place* all of the following:
- 28 detailed lesson plans with suggested tasks, timings and groupings
- stimulus texts and pictures
- worksheets and handouts for students
- suggested answers where appropriate
- task tips and response guidance in plans and answers
- accompanying CD-ROM.

The pages are all photocopiable for classroom use. The accompanying CD-ROM contains pdfs of the texts which can be digitally projected, hot links to websites, colour visuals and slideshows, worksheets in both Word and pdf format, plus additional information (checklists, success criteria, tips, processes and writing structures) for quick reference or distribution to students.

Success in the First Language English examination depends on skills development, adequate preparation for the types of question, familiarity with the way responses are assessed, coverage of the syllabus, and careful lesson planning by teachers to ensure maximum focus, motivation and production by students. All of these criteria are satisfied by the *Teacher's Resource*, and because it provides teaching ideas as well as the necessary resources, the teacher has only to concentrate on effective delivery of the lesson. The various genres of reading passages or writing tasks likely to be set in the exam are all included (letter, report, news report, magazine article, travel writing, speech, dialogue), as are the types of writing set in the composition paper or for the coursework portfolio: informative, argument, discursive, descriptive and narrative.

The resource covers the skills of skim-reading for gist, scan-reading for data identification, selecting, modifying, developing, paraphrasing, summarising, structuring, sequencing, supporting and argument evaluation. It also stresses throughout the importance of understanding implicit (as well as explicit) meaning, making inferences, recognising writers' devices when reading, and the consideration of voice, audience, register, purpose, and the adoption of an appropriate style and accuracy of expression when writing. Each unit includes all or most of the Assessment Objectives for Reading (4), Writing (5) and Speaking and Listening (5), so that there is continual practice and reinforcement of the objectives across a range of tasks and topics. There are speaking and listening opportunities in every unit, some of which can be assessed for exam purposes.

## Using the resource

The *Teacher's Resource* book is divided into six parts, one for each type of written exam question across the four components. It contains **28 units**, each providing tasks for one double lesson plus homework and optional additional activities. The units are not progressive and can be completed in any order to match the syllabus options selected and the structure of the departmental scheme of work in each centre. Used in conjunction with the coursebook, workbook and past papers, the resource provides more than enough material for a two-year (five-term) course.

At the start of each unit is a **topic outline box,** indicating the skill, exam-question type and outcome particularly focused on in that unit. In the interests of good teaching methodology and student motivation, other related tasks are included for variety and integration of the four main skills areas (reading, writing, speaking and listening). Asterisks denote outcomes (i.e. the pieces of work produced by the students, which each take the form of an exam-style response) covered by optional additional tasks. There are also opportunities for the practice, revisiting and reinforcement of the specific language skills of style, structure, sentence structure, vocabulary extension and mechanical accuracy.

Every unit has a complete **lesson plan** for the teacher, with detailed and sequenced **tasks**. There is an average of 12 tasks per unit, ensuring variety of resources, groupings, feedback methods and outcomes. The plan includes advice on how the tasks should be completed (as an individual, paired, small-group or whole-class activity), the form of the feedback (spoken or written, volunteered or requested), and how it should be assessed (self, peer, class or teacher).

The lesson plan is followed by the **texts** (for teacher and students), typically either two or three per unit, some of which may be visual. Some units also contain **worksheets** or **handouts** for the students. At the end of each unit are **answers** (for the teacher), indicating the kind of response to be expected for those tasks which can have generic responses.

Most units contain a minimum of two texts of between 600 and 800 words, to reflect the format of the Extended tier of the Reading paper in the exam (the Core tier has one such passage), linked by topic to give coherence and to reflect the thematic linking of the Paper 2 exam passages. These passages provide a range of genres to reflect the types of texts likely to be used in the exam papers, and to supply models for the different types of writing response required. Covering all continents and a wide range of countries, the passages have an international flavour, while the choice of topics has youth appeal.

The **timings** in the lesson plans (in brackets in multiples of 5 minutes) are necessarily approximate, since they will be affected by the number of students in the class. A 90-minute lesson can easily be divided into three if shorter lessons are required, or extended to two hours by the setting of the **additional task**, or by the starting of the **homework task** within the lesson. It is often possible to borrow time from one task to give to another, or to leave out some tasks completely if time is short. The longer writing tasks, providing the main exam-skill practice, are set for homework as they require up to an hour to complete, depending on type, and should be done independently.

The additional tasks can be used as extension activities for individual students who finish early or who need to be stretched. Thus the lesson plans are flexible and adaptable, enabling the teacher to tailor them to the size, ability and working speed of the class, and to give them the emphasis required for a particular task, discussion or feedback.

It is hoped that the *Teacher's Resource* will be inspirational to both teachers and students in the breadth and abundance of its topics and tasks. Through its close focus on exam skills and assessment criteria, as well as on the fundamental skills that students need to become competent users of English, it should prove an invaluable aid to good teaching and learning.

## Notes

- Where texts are of American origin the original spelling has been retained. Candidates may use either British or American spelling in their writing, provided that they are consistent.

- The websites given in the web links page on the CD-ROM have all been found useful. The publisher cannot guarantee the persistence or accuracy of URLs for external or third-party internet websites.

- It is assumed that teachers will provide students with the Generic Mark Scheme grids (link to CIE website provided on the CD-ROM), as advised by CIE, so that assessment comments can include phrases from the descriptors to enable students to become familiar with and clear about what is required for each part of the exam, and how the assessment objectives relate to the tasks and their marking criteria.

- Students are advised in the lesson plans to use highlighters – sometimes in different colours – to annotate texts for passage-based questions, as an aid to close focus on reading and easy selection of material for planning. Some centres have misunderstood the rubric on the front of the 0500 exam papers which says 'Do not use staples, paper clips, highlighters, glue or correction fluid'. This refers only to the answer papers to be sent to CIE for assessment, and does not refer to what candidates are allowed to do to their question papers in the exam room. The use of highlighting or underlining is good practice in the exam and to be encouraged as a classroom habit throughout the course.

- Lesson tasks are addressed to the teacher using the self-instructional style commonly used in lesson plans, whereas the homework tasks are in a form which enables them to be set for students without modification, either orally or in writing on the board.

# Skills and tasks

|  | Paper 1; Paper 2 Question 1 | Paper 1; Paper 2 Question 2 | Paper 1; Paper 2 Question 3 | Paper 3 part 1 | Paper 3 part 2 Coursework 1 & 3 | Paper 3 part 2 Coursework 2 |
|---|---|---|---|---|---|---|
|  | **comprehension** | **writer's effect** | **summary** | **directed writing** | **argumentative discursive** | **descriptive imaginative** |
|  | vocabulary paraphrasing inferring selecting | connotations style analysis | complex sentences | collating register genre transformation sequencing voice | persuasive informative structure rhetoric detecting bias evaluating | structure imagery character setting |
| Unit 1 | ✓✓ | ✓ | ✓ | ✓ | ✓✓ | ✓ |
| Unit 2 | ✓ | ✓ | ✓ | ✓ |  | ✓ |
| Unit 3 | ✓ | ✓ | ✓(✓) | ✓ |  |  |
| Unit 4 | ✓ | ✓✓✓ |  | ✓ | ✓(✓)(✓) | ✓ |
| Unit 5 |  | ✓✓✓ |  |  |  | ✓(✓) |
| Unit 6 | ✓ | ✓ |  |  |  | ✓✓ |
| Unit 7 | ✓✓ | ✓✓ |  |  |  | ✓ |
| Unit 8 | ✓✓ | ✓✓✓✓ |  |  |  | ✓✓(✓) |
| Unit 9 | ✓✓✓✓ |  | ✓✓ | ✓ |  |  |
| Unit 10 | ✓ |  | ✓✓✓ | ✓ | ✓ |  |
| Unit 11 |  |  | ✓✓ |  |  |  |
| Unit 12 |  |  | ✓✓✓ |  | ✓(✓) |  |
| Unit 13 | ✓✓ |  |  | ✓✓ |  |  |
| Unit 14 | ✓✓ |  | (✓) | ✓✓✓ |  |  |
| Unit 15 |  |  | ✓ | ✓✓ | ✓ |  |
| Unit 16 | ✓ | ✓ | ✓ | ✓✓ | ✓✓✓(✓) |  |
| Unit 17 | ✓ |  | ✓ | ✓ | ✓✓✓✓(✓)(✓) |  |
| Unit 18 |  |  | ✓✓✓ |  | ✓✓✓(✓) |  |
| Unit 19 |  | ✓ |  |  |  | ✓✓✓ |
| Unit 20 |  |  |  |  |  | ✓✓✓(✓) |
| Unit 21 |  |  |  |  |  |  |
| Unit 22 | ✓ |  | ✓ |  |  | ✓✓ |
| Unit 23 |  | ✓ |  | ✓ | ✓ |  |
| Unit 24 | ✓ |  | ✓✓ |  | ✓✓ |  |
| Unit 25 | ✓ |  |  |  | ✓ | ✓✓ |
| Unit 26 |  |  |  |  |  | ✓✓✓(✓)(✓) |
| Unit 27 |  |  |  |  | ✓✓✓(✓) |  |
| Unit 28 |  |  |  | ✓ | ✓✓✓✓ |  |

**Notes**
The skills are shown along the top of the grid, under the syllabus component in which they feature.
✓ indicates that a skill is covered in a particular unit.

| | Paper 3 part 2 Coursework 2 | Paper 1; Paper 2; Paper 3 | Paper 1; Paper 2; Paper 3 | Paper 1; Paper 2; Paper 3 | Paper 1; Paper 2; Paper 3; Paper 5/ Paper 6 | Paper 1; Paper 2; Paper 3; Paper 5/ Paper 6 |
|---|---|---|---|---|---|---|
| | **narrative** | letter website blog diary appeal | journalism news report magazine article broadcast leaflet advertisement | report review travel writing | dialogue role play interview discussion | speech debate talk monologue |
| | structure use of dialogue persona viewpoint | | | | | |
| 1 | | ✓ | ✓ | ✓ | | |
| 2 | | | ✓ | | ✓ | |
| 3 | | | ✓ | (✓) | ✓ | |
| 4 | | (✓) | | ✓✓ | | |
| 5 | ✓✓ | | | | ✓ | |
| 6 | ✓(✓) | ✓ | | | ✓ | |
| 7 | | | | | | |
| 8 | | | | | | |
| 9 | (✓) | | ✓ | | | |
| 10 | | | ✓ | | ✓(✓) | |
| 11 | | | ✓✓ | | (✓)(✓) | |
| 12 | | | ✓ | | (✓) | |
| 13 | | | | | ✓ | ✓✓(✓) |
| 14 | | ✓ | (✓) | | ✓ | |
| 15 | | (✓) | | ✓ | ✓(✓) | ✓ |
| 16 | | ✓ | (✓) | | ✓(✓) | |
| 17 | | ✓ | | | ✓ | ✓(✓) |
| 18 | | | | | ✓ | ✓ |
| 19 | | | | | | (✓) |
| 20 | | | | | | |
| 21 | ✓✓✓(✓) | | | | | |
| 22 | ✓✓✓✓(✓) | | | | | |
| 23 | ✓ | | ✓ | | | ✓(✓) |
| 24 | | | | (✓) | ✓✓ | |
| 25 | | ✓ | | | ✓ | (✓) |
| 26 | | | | | | ✓ |
| 27 | | | | | ✓ | (✓) |
| 28 | | ✓ | | | | ✓ |

More than one ✓ indicates the number of tasks/outcomes for that skill within the same unit.
(✓) indicates tasks set as additional (and therefore optional) tasks.

# Terms and conditions of use for the CD-ROM

This is a legal agreement between 'You' (which means the individual customer or the Educational Institution and its authorised users) and Cambridge University Press ('the Licensor') for *Cambridge IGCSE First Language English Teacher's Resource CD-ROM*. By placing this CD in the CD-ROM drive of your computer, You agree to the terms of this licence.

**1 Limited licence**

a You are purchasing only the right to use the CD-ROM and are acquiring no rights, express or implied, to it, other than those rights granted in this limited licence for not-for-profit educational use only.

b The Licensor grants You the licence to use one copy of this CD-ROM.

c You shall not: (**i**) copy or authorise copying of the CD-ROM, (**ii**) translate the CD-ROM, (**iii**) reverse-engineer, alter, adapt, disassemble or decompile the CD-ROM, (**iv**) transfer, sell, lease, lend, profit from, assign or otherwise convey all or any portion of the CD-ROM or (**v**) operate the CD-ROM from a mainframe system, except as provided in these terms and conditions.

d Permission is explicitly granted for use of the CD-ROM on a data projector, interactive whiteboard or other public display in the context of classroom teaching at a purchasing institution.

e If You are an Educational Institution, once a teacher ceases to be a member of the Educational Institution, all copies of the material on the CD-ROM stored on his/her personal computer must be destroyed and the CD-ROM returned to the Educational Institution.

f You are permitted to print reasonable copies of the printable resources on the CD-ROM. These must be used solely for use within the context of classroom teaching at a purchasing institution.

**2 Copyright**

a All original content is provided as part of the CD-ROM (including text, images and ancillary material) and is the copyright of the Licensor or has been licensed to the Licensor for use in the CD-ROM, protected by copyright and all other applicable intellectual-property laws and international treaties.

b You may not copy the CD-ROM except for making one copy of the CD-ROM solely for backup or archival purposes. You may not alter, remove or destroy any copyright notice or other material placed on or with this CD-ROM.

**3 Liability and Indemnification**

a The CD-ROM is supplied 'as is' with no express guarantee as to its suitability. To the extent permitted by applicable law, the Licensor is not liable for costs of procurement of substitute products, damages or losses of any kind whatsoever resulting from the use of this product, or errors or faults in the CD-ROM, and in every case the Licensor's liability shall be limited to the suggested list price or the amount actually paid by You for the product, whichever is lower.

b You accept that the Licensor is not responsible for the availability of any links within or outside the CD-ROM and that the Licensor is not responsible or liable for any content available from sources outside the CD-ROM to which such links are made.

c Where, through use of the original material, You infringe the copyright of the Licensor, You undertake to indemnify and keep indemnified the Licensor from and against any loss, cost, damage or expense (including without limitation damages paid to a third party and any reasonable legal costs) incurred by the Licensor as a result of such infringement.

**4 Termination**

Without prejudice to any other rights, the Licensor may terminate this licence if You fail to comply with the terms and conditions of the licence. In such an event, You must destroy all copies of the CD-ROM.

**5 Governing law**

This agreement is governed by the laws of England, without regard to its 'conflict of laws' provision, and each party irrevocably submits to the exclusive jurisdiction of the English courts. The parties disclaim the application of the United Nations Convention of the International Sale of Goods.

# Responding to reading

## Unit 1 Taking a break

**Topic outline**

- **Syllabus component:** Paper 1; Paper 2 questions 1 and 2
- **Main skills:** responding to reading; reading for inference; reading for effects
- **Secondary skills:** summary; persuasive writing; descriptive writing
- **Outcome:** informal letter; persuasive speech; *advertisement
- **Materials:** holiday advertisements
- **Texts:** Text 1A: Cruising the Caribbean; Text 1B: Europe express

## Lesson plan

1 Ask students to skim-read Text 1A. (5)

2 What do people appear to want on holiday? Students work in pairs and make a list of inferences from Text 1A. (5)

3 Collect feedback. (5)

4 Ask students to scan Text 1A for persuasive advertising devices and to underline them. (5)

5 Collect feedback and list on the board. Discuss as a class why the devices are effective. (10)

6 Ask students to list the points from Text 1A which could be used to summarise the attractions of a) a cruise and b) *Sea Cloud II*. (5)

7 Collect points on the board so students can add to their lists if necessary. (5)

8 Set a writing task: Imagine you are on a *Sea Cloud II* Caribbean cruise with your family and you are writing a letter to a friend from the ship. Students use their list of points to write about a page, adding details and inferences to develop the ideas in Text 1A. (15)

9 Ask students, in pairs, to check each other's letters for appropriateness and accuracy. Collect letters to assess for a) use of material (15 marks), and b) style and structure (5 marks). (5)

10 Choose three students to each read out an option in Text 1B. Students then scan the text and underline all the adjectives to do with sight. (5)

11 Which adjectives are the most evocative? Ask students to evaluate and order the adjectives from the least to the most evocative. Invite students to justify their order, and discuss as a class. (5)

12 What kind of person does each of the three holidays appeal to? Ask students to write a few sentences as a profile for the sort of holidaymaker they infer would be attracted to the three destinations in Text 1B. (10)

13 Ask students to read out their profiles and justify their inferences. (10)

## Homework task

Your parents are trying to decide between a cruise and a railway trip for the next family holiday. Using ideas from Texts 1A and 1B, write what you would say to persuade them to choose whichever holiday you would prefer.

## Additional task

Ask students to work in small groups to produce a one-page holiday advertisement for a national magazine. Encourage them to use a word processor to incorporate a variety of attractive fonts, boxes, shapes and colours, and allow them to use imported graphics. The advertisement should employ some of the structural and stylistic features of Texts 1A and 1B, and should include information about transport, trips itinerary and accommodation.

# Text 1A

# Cruising the Caribbean

There is something quite magical about exploring the islands of the Caribbean Sea aboard a tall ship. But what makes this trip uniquely fascinating is the opportunity to sail aboard the most luxurious tall ship in the world. Join us aboard *Sea Cloud II* at the most perfect time of year to escape our northern climes for two weeks of warm weather sailing through the West Indies.

Join us for a voyage of discovery aboard this most elegant of ships and experience the elation of travelling under sail as we island hop across the Caribbean. Every island is different, each with its own character. Some mountainous and lush, some low lying and arid, but all with their own distinct charm. In the main we will avoid the larger and better known islands in favour of the smaller and less developed. After all, the major delight of a trip aboard the *Sea Cloud II* is to drop anchor off a remote island and enjoy the beauty and peace of the surroundings as far away from the crowds as possible.

Launched in 2001, *Sea Cloud II* is a stunning vessel, built along traditional lines, but offering deluxe accommodation. Built to accommodate 96 passengers in five star luxury, she offers a range of beautifully appointed suites and cabins which are furnished with great style. All accommodations have outside views and the bathrooms, in light marble, are unusually spacious and extremely comfortable. The finest, carefully chosen fabrics, combined with leather, rattan and other materials, brass and gold, precious woods and marble together create an impressive ensemble. No expense has been spared to create a sympathetic ambience in both the accommodations and public areas, and this is reflected throughout the vessel. Public areas include an elegant lounge, library, fitness centre, boutique, pool, bar and hospital. The single sitting dining room is airy and modern and the quality of the cuisine and service will be to the highest of standards, as one would expect on a *Sea Cloud* cruise. Relax on the lido deck and experience the natural grandeur of travelling under sail, as 30,000 square feet of sail rekindles memories of a bygone age.

Source: www.noble-caledonia.co.uk

**Text 1B**

# Europe express

## The enchanting shores of Lake Garda

Relax and unwind on our 8-day escorted holiday on the shores of enchanting Lake Garda with a few carefully chosen excursions, based on the beautiful peninsula close to historic Sirmione. Highlights of the holiday include:

- A comfortable lakeside hotel with pool
- Delightful views of Lake Garda from the hotel's pretty gardens
- The attractions of Sirmione, with its *gelaterias*, boutiques, 13th-century castle and Roman villa
- Our included cruise on Lake Garda with visit to a traditional market
- Our optional trip to classical Verona, setting for Shakespeare's *Romeo and Juliet*
- The charms of romantic Venice, with guided tour and dinner, on our optional excursion

**8 days from 600 euros**
12 departures: 12 April to 18 October

## Historic Vienna, Prague & Berlin

Here is the perfect chance to savour the majesty of Eastern Europe's captivating capital cities. Highlights of the holiday include:

- A 10-day escorted grand tour staying in three fascinating European cities
- Well-located and comfortable 4-star hotels
- A night on the Cologne to Vienna CityNightLine sleeper train
- Our included walking tours of charming Prague and beautiful Dresden
- Included city tours of imperial Vienna and fascinating Berlin
- An optional trip to the famous Schönbrunn Palace and its elegant, formal gardens
- Optional visit to Potsdam with its Prussian and German palaces set in stunning gardens

**10 days from 850 euros**
6 departures: 8 May to 9 October

## Little trains of the Rhine Valley

Discover the attractions of the romantic Rhine Valley as we take relaxing trips amidst the winding rivers, vineyards and fairytale castles on our 5-day escorted holiday. Highlights of the holiday include:

- Friendly, family-run hotel in riverside Remagen
- Our included tour through the beautiful Ahr Valley with the opportunity to sample the region's wonderful wines and enjoy a horse-drawn carriage ride
- An optional excursion to the historic riverside town of Königswinter and a trip by funicular railway high up to the Drachenfels rocky outcrop above
- Our included scenic excursion through the dramatic Rhine Gorge to the charming wine town of Rüdesheim

**5 days from 400 euros**
8 departures: 18 May to 5 October

Source: www.treynholidays.co.uk

# Answers – Unit 1

**2** Text 1A: what people want on holiday:
- magic
- unique experience
- warm weather
- discovery
- variety
- unspoilt places
- unknown places
- tranquillity
- luxury accommodation
- good views
- spacious bathrooms
- attractive furniture / ambience
- range of facilities
- to dine in one sitting
- good food
- relaxation
- feeling of returning to the past

**5** Text 1A: persuasive devices:

**adjectives** – nouns qualified by at least one adjective to stress attractions, e.g. **precious** woods, **natural** grandeur

**adverbs** – adjectives modified by adverbs to intensify them, e.g. **unusually** spacious and **extremely** comfortable, **uniquely** fascinating

**euphemisms** – make things sound more luxurious and spacious, e.g. accommodations for cabins, vessel for boat, boutique for shop

**clichés** – evoke stock responses and don't require thought, e.g. No expense has been spared, five star luxury

**French words** – sound more grand and exotic, e.g. deluxe, ensemble, ambience, grandeur

**repetition** – has an insistent effect, and is especially used for key names like Sea Cloud

**archaisms** – give the impression of an 'olde worlde' charm, e.g. in the main for mainly, appointed for decorated, bygone for past, elation for joy, aboard, rekindles, accommodations in the plural

**superlatives**, e.g. the most perfect, this most elegant of ships

**lists** – give impression of abundance of sensory pleasures

**prolixity** – more words sound more impressive, e.g. to the highest of standards instead of good quality

**use of first person plural** – we includes reader and seems friendly

**use of future tense** – implies that reader will have this experience soon

**imperatives** – commands aim to coerce the reader, as in hypnotism, to imagine being there and thus fall under the spell of the advert, e.g. Join us, Relax on the lido deck

**6** Text 1A: summary points:

**a** The cruise
- is romantic
- is comfortable
- is an elegant way to travel
- is able to visit islands
- can go to remote inaccessible places
- can avoid crowds of tourists

**b** *Sea Cloud II*
- is new
- is built in a traditional style
- has deluxe accommodation
- is decorated with many kinds of expensive substances and fabrics
- has lots of things to do on board
- has medical facilities
- has excellent cuisine
- has large sails like old-fashioned sailing ships

**11** Text 1B: adjectival rank order:

These adjectives are all vague clichés, and all mean more or less the same thing, but they are always used in the context of visual pleasure and so are beloved of advertisers. Their power decreases in proportion to the frequency of their usage in everyday expression, and increases in proportion to their associations with putting someone under a spell, so the ascending order of evocativeness for these words is probably: *beautiful, delightful, romantic, charming, fascinating, enchanting, captivating, stunning*.

**12** Text 1B: customer profiles:

Lake Garda: this holiday suits people who work in cities who need to go somewhere in the countryside to relax. They like to have everything arranged for them so that no decisions need to be taken about visits. They are quite interested in historic sites and cultural events, but they also like to spend days doing nothing but sitting by the hotel pool, getting a tan and enjoying the peaceful natural landscape. Shopping opportunities are something they also take advantage of. This holiday attracts younger people who are on a limited budget and don't want to spend more than they have to on their travel and accommodation. Because this trip's season starts earlier than the others and goes on longer, it appeals to those seeking somewhere warmer in spring and autumn or those who like off-peak breaks.

Capital cities: people who choose this holiday are energetic and like the idea of seeing a lot of different places in a short time. The climate is not a concern for them. They are particularly interested in architecture and history, and want a guide with them to tell them about the buildings they are looking at to make the trip informative. They are walkers and enjoyers of gardens. They like unusual experiences and being busy, but they also like to be comfortable at the end of the day. The clients on this trip tend to be middle-aged and quite well off. They know what they want and are prepared to pay a bit more to get their perfect holiday.

Rhine valley: this holiday is for railway enthusiasts and those who enjoy river scenery. It also attracts those who like German wines. The accommodation is modest and personal, and does not appeal to those who prefer to stay in luxury hotels. The old-fashioned modes of transport and leisurely pace of the travel cater for the elderly and less athletic client. The trip visits only small towns and would not suit those looking for bustling city life and grand architecture, or those who just want to stay at the hotel enjoying its facilities. This is a medium-priced holiday for those who cannot afford to be extravagant but who are not bargain hunting.

# Responding to reading

## Unit 2 The falling wall

**Topic outline**

- **Syllabus component:** Paper 1; Paper 2 questions 1 and 2
- **Main skills:** comprehension; developing a response to reading
- **Secondary skills:** identifying writers' effects; complex sentences; genre transformation; interviewing
- **Outcome:** news report; *descriptive writing
- **Materials:** short story; news report structure handout
- **Text:** Text 2: Framed

## Lesson plan

1  Choose students to each read out part of Text 2. (5)

2  Ask students, in pairs, to underline words and phrases which convey:
   a  the power of the water in paragraphs 1, 2 and 3.
   b  the power of the fire in paragraphs 4 and 5.
   c  the power of the wall in paragraphs 1, 3 and 5. (5)

3  Invite answers and comments on why the choices are effective. (10)

4  Ask students to join into complex sentences:
   a  the four simple sentences at the beginning of paragraph 4.
   b  the four simple sentences in the final paragraph.
   Ask what difference this makes to the story. (It alters the emphasis, stresses cause and effect, and speeds up the narrative pace.) (10)

5  Choose students to read out their answers. Discuss and evaluate as a class. (5)

6  Allocate roles to the students: one of the three surviving firemen to the most articulate students, reporter to the others. Ask them to use Text 2 to prepare for a press conference, the reporters each thinking of a different question, the firemen of their answers. Go around the class, prompting where necessary. (10)

7  Hold a press conference at which the firemen take turns to answer questions and reporters take notes of their answers. (10)

8  Ask students to plan a news report of the event (see CD-ROM for news report structure handout), including statements by an eye witness and an official. They should use information from their press conference notes as well as Text 2. Encourage them to create additional 'factual' details such as names and ages of people and places. (15)

9  Elicit the features of news report style and list on the board (include short paragraphs, short sentences, short words, sensational vocabulary, statistical facts, adjective strings before the noun). Ask students to write the first two paragraphs for their report, including these features. (5)

10  Choose students to read out their paragraphs for the class to evaluate. (5)

11  What makes a good headline? Write examples of headlines on the board and ask students to define the characteristics of headlines. (Elicit 'telegram' language i.e. 1–6 words, short words, no articles, present tense; alliteration, assonance or puns are optional.) (5)

12  Ask students to suggest headlines for their own news report and, in pairs, decide on the best one. (5)

## Homework task

Write the news report of the fire and collapse of the wall. Give the report a headline and a sub-heading within the report.

## Additional task

Ask students to write a description of a building on fire, using similes, metaphors and multiple adjectives in their writing.

# Text 2

# Framed

*The writer and his fire-fighting colleagues are putting out a fire in a warehouse in London, caused by an air-raid bomb, when there is an accident.*

I remember it was our third job that night, and it was 3 a.m. And there we were – Len, Lofty, Verno and myself, playing a fifty-foot jet up the face of a tall city warehouse and thinking nothing at all. You don't think of anything after the first few hours. You just watch the white pole of water lose itself in the fire and you think of nothing. Sometimes you move the jet over to another window. Sometimes the orange dims to black, but you only ease your grip on the ice-cold nozzle and continue pouring careless gallons through the window. You know the fire will fester for hours yet. However, that night the blank, indefinite hours of waiting were sharply interrupted by an unusual sound. Very suddenly a long rattling crack of bursting brick and mortar perforated the moment. And then the upper half of that five-storey building heaved over towards us. It hung there, poised for a timeless second before rumbling down at us. I was thinking of nothing at all and then I was thinking of everything in the world.

In that simple second my brain digested every detail of the scene. New eyes opened at the sides of my head so that, from within, I photographed a hemispherical panorama bounded by the huge length of the building in front of me and the narrow lane on either side. Blocking us on the left was the squat pump, roaring and quivering with effort. Water throbbed from its overflow valves and from leakages in the hose. A ceaseless stream spewed down its grey sides into the gutter. To the other side of me was a free run up the alley. A couple of lengths of dead, deflated hose wound over the darkly glistening pavement. A needle of water fountained from a hole in a live hose.

Behind me, Len and Verno shared the weight of the hose. They heaved up against the strong backward drag of water pressure. All I had to do was yell 'Drop it!' and then run. We could risk the live hose snaking up at us. We could run to the right down the free alley – Len, Verno and me. But I never moved. That long second held me hypnotized, rubber boots cemented to the pavement. Ton upon ton of red-hot brick hovering in the air above us numbed all initiative.

The building was five storeys high. The top four storeys were fiercely alight. The rooms inside were alive with red fire. The black outside walls remained untouched. And thus, like the lighted carriages of a night express train, there appeared alternating rectangles of black and red that emphasized vividly the extreme symmetry of the window spacing. Orange-red colour seemed to bulge from the black framework like boiling jelly that expanded inside a thick black squared grill.

Three of the storeys, thirty blazing windows and their huge frame of black brick, a hundred solid tons of hard, deep Victorian wall, pivoted over towards us and hung flatly over the alley. The night grew darker as the great mass hung over us and the moonlight was shut out. The picture appeared static to the limited surface sense, but beyond that there was hidden movement. A wall will fall in many ways. It may sway over to the one side or the other. It may crumble at the very beginning of its fall. It may remain intact and fall flat. This wall fell as flat as a pancake. It clung to its shape through ninety degrees to the horizontal. Then it detached itself from the pivot and slammed down on top of us, cracking like automatic gunfire. The violent sound both deafened us and brought us to our senses. We dropped the hose and crouched. Afterwards Verno said that I knelt slowly on one knee with bowed head, like a man about to be knighted. Well, I got my knighting. There was an incredible noise – a thunderclap condensed into the space of an eardrum – and then the bricks and mortar came tearing and burning into the flesh of my face.

Lofty, by the pump, was killed. Len, Verno and myself they dug out. There was very little brick on top of us. We had been lucky. We had been framed by one of those symmetrical, rectangular window spaces.

**Adapted from 'The Wall' by William Samsom, in *Fireman Flower*, The Vanguard Press, 1945.**

# Answers – Unit 2

**2a** Power of the water:

*fifty-foot jet* – height of water and the pressure implied by *jet*

*pole of water* – height of water and its rigidity

*careless gallons* – amount of water, as if it was inexhaustible

*water throbbed* – describes pulsing effect of the bursts of water and the action of the pump

*ceaseless stream spewed* – emphasises unending quantity and the way it was gushing out

*fountained* – shows height and pressure

*strong backward drag of water pressure* – force of water in the hose

*the live hose snaking up* – like a dangerous reptile capable of rising up and striking because of the power of water inside; it sustains the metaphor begun by *live*, *dead* and *wound*

**2b** Power of the fire:

*fiercely alight* – makes it clear that the fire is violent and threatening

*alive with red fire* – fire has animated the building, making it dangerous and unpredictable

*a night express train* – the building has been turned into an unstoppable force

*bulge* – unpleasant word depicting how the fire moves and distorts

*like boiling jelly* – refers to both its extreme heat and its capacity to melt things in its path

*thirty blazing windows* – the fire can light up a huge expanse of building at the same time

**2c** Power of the wall:

*a long rattling crack of bursting brick and mortar perforated the moment* – the noise of the wall breaking up is like gunfire; the verb is a destructive one of making holes

*building heaved over towards us* – as if alive it moved its gigantic weight to threaten the men

*Ton upon ton of red-hot brick hovering in the air* – an inordinate weight of fiery bricks were just hanging like a bird of prey, waiting to plunge and kill those below

*pivoted over towards us* – had the power to twist itself and pursue the target

*a hundred solid tons* – emphasises weight and density

*the great mass hung over us and the moonlight was shut out* – the sheer size of the falling wall created a fearful darkness overhead

*slammed down on top of us* – the verb is one of destructive force

*cracking like automatic gunfire* – noise is again mentioned; the simile again equates the wall with a deadly weapon

*a thunderclap* – compares the noise of the falling wall to the deafening noise of a storm overhead (sustaining the metaphor of *rumbling* in paragraph 1)

*the bricks and mortar came tearing and burning* – shows the wall's violent movement and speed, and the damage it is about to inflict

# Responding to reading

## Unit 3 The gentle touch

**Topic outline**

- **Syllabus component:** Paper 1; Paper 2 question 1
- **Main skills:** comprehension; response to reading
- **Secondary skills:** selecting material; developing material; recognising style
- **Outcome:** magazine article; summary; *film review
- **Materials:** newspaper article; Worksheet for Text 3: Monty's method; review writing structure handout
- **Text:** Text 3: Monty's method

## Lesson plan

1. Read Text 3 aloud to the class. (5)

2. Give out Worksheet for Text 3 and ask students to complete it. (20)

3. Tell students to swap worksheets and give out answers while students mark each other's work. Collect marks (out of 30). (10)

4. Ask students, working individually and silently, to plan and write a response to the following task: You are interviewing Monty Roberts on a TV chat show. Write the replies he gives to the following questions:

   a How would you describe the 'magic' that you perform at public events?

   b What are your beliefs about horses and children?

   c Why do you think you are so successful at what you do?

   Students should write between a page and a page and a half of average-sized writing. (25)

5. Ask students, in pairs, to read and comment on each other's work, then to add, delete, improve and correct their own. Collect responses for assessment (Reading mark out of 15, Writing mark out of 5). (5)

6. What sort of text is Text 3? Ask students, in pairs, to identify the characteristics of the genre of Text 3, which is a mixture of news reporting and magazine article. (5)

7. Collect feedback and list on board, explaining the purpose of the characteristics. (5)

8. Ask students to plan an article for their school magazine, describing Monty's methods and how they can be applied in schools. Make sure they understand that they should scan the passage, select the material they will use and organise a structure for it in their plans. (Write the acronym VARP on the board – voice, audience, register, purpose – as a reminder for students.) (10)

9. Go around the class, advising on and approving plans. (5)

## Homework task

Write your magazine article, beginning *The school trip to see Monty Roberts was not only highly entertaining but has caused us to reflect on the way students are treated in schools.* Remember to modify the language, voice, focus and style for the genre and audience of a school magazine article.

## Additional tasks

a Ask students to research on the Internet the life story of Monty Roberts and select key points in order to write his biography so far.

b Ask students to watch the film *The Horse Whisperer*, based on the life and methods of Monty Roberts. They should take notes while viewing, and afterwards write a review of the film (see CD-ROM for review writing structure handout).

Text 3

# Monty's method

*Monty is the real-life Californian Horse Whisperer who can train a mustang to accept a saddle and rider in 10 minutes.*

On a cold Tuesday night in September, 1000 people are gathering in a barn the size of an aircraft hangar. In the queue, there's a man covered in blue denim from Stetson to cowboy boots whose spurs rattle as he walks. He looks the part. They are all here to see Monty Roberts. Outside, one of the volunteers who is putting up signs says 'In the horse world, he's a bit of a god.'

Monty Roberts is also gaining something of a reputation in the world of education as schools start to apply his **techniques** in the classroom. His theories on non-confrontational human relationships have been **credited with** turning round failing schools.

Back in the barn, the warm-up music of classic western themes fades and the night's star attraction appears. A big bear of a man with a gentle smile, he **acknowledges** the applause and walks into the fenced pen at the centre of the arena. 'Practically everybody here has read or heard something about me,' he begins. 'That's just the way it is today. But there won't be one horse who comes through that gate tonight that has read or heard anything about me.'

The first horse to enter the arena is a handsome animal called Socks. Like a magician about to perform a trick, Monty asks Socks's owner if they have ever met. He needs to rule out any **collusion** because what follows is so magical as to beggar belief. But it is not a trick. Socks is a 'starter', meaning he has never been ridden. In fact, he has never had anything on his back. He is wild – in the top 5 per cent of untrained horses. Socks starts to run round the pen, first one way then the other, as Monty throws a line softly on to his back and kicks up sawdust and dirt, **imitating** a predator. After a couple of minutes, Socks realises he is not in danger and starts to chew and lick his lips, just as Monty said he would. Then he stops, and drops his head to the ground.

And then the magic begins. Monty stands sideways on and walks slowly towards Socks, avoiding eye contact. Then Socks turns towards him, and Monty **scurries** away. This is not the action of a predator, the horse thinks. The third time he does this, something incredible happens. Socks begins to follow Monty across the ring, his head almost resting on his shoulder. In eight minutes, wild horse and civilised man have made friends, achieving what Monty calls 'join-up'. He signals for his rider to bring a saddle, and within 10 minutes Socks is carrying a man on his back around the ring. 'Horses are stupid – that's what they said for 2000 years. Look at this young horse. Look at him learn. Horses are 50 million years old, and humans have been around for a much shorter period of time. Horses have been my teachers as much as I have been theirs.'

Monty Roberts has done this routine thousands of times. It's second nature to him. It's the reason he's famous. But it's not his *raison d'être*. During the evening he will 'join up' with five horses, gently curing them of habits of biting and bucking and refusing to go into boxes or through gates, without laying a finger on them except to pat their noses. But incredible though this is, it is only a sideshow.

Monty's main concern these days is to apply his non-violent methods to human relationships, to **revolutionise** the way we communicate. 'These are the most precious relationships,' he says. 'Every human being is more precious than all the horses I have worked with.' Like horses, children are flight animals, meaning that when threatened they flee, except that our predatory ancestry means we put up with a lot more abuse before we run. 'Each of the animals that comes in that pen is just like a child,' says Monty. 'They have the same needs. They want trust, they want to be able to trust, they want safety and some love. They don't want to be hurt.'

His philosophy is simple: positive actions reap positive consequences; negative actions incur negative consequences. He encourages parents and children to draw up a series of contracts, verbal or written, and this gives even children as young as two a sense of responsibility. Children should never be rewarded for good behaviour with food or money, but allowed to go on an outing or do a favourite pastime instead. Breaking the contract means a task, but this should be something useful. It is important that the child decides on both the reward and the task and that both parties stick to the deal. 'There's not a bad kid born,' says Monty. 'There's not a bad horse born. Circumstances and life's environment are what make us either bad or good. And teachers have been the most important part of our sociological order since the beginning of time, because they represent what our future will be.'

Monty is a **charismatic**, articulate but modest man. He describes his work as a mission to leave the world a better place than he found it. In some places, in prisons and schools, thanks to him, it already is.

Adapted from Harvey McGavin, *Times Educational Supplement*, 21st September 2001.

# Worksheet for Text 3: Monty's method

1  Explain in your own words *He looks the part*.  [1]

2  Explain the meaning of *In the horse world he's a bit of a god*.  [1]

3  Why does Monty say that no horses have read or heard about him?  [2]

4  Explain, using your own words, what the writer means by:  **[1 mark each: 3]**

   a  *so magical as to beggar belief*

   b  *It's second nature to him.*

   c  *it is only a sideshow*

5  Give another word for each of the following bolded words.  **[1 mark each: 8]**

   a  *techniques*

   b  *credited with*

   c  *acknowledges*

   d  *collusion*

   e  *imitating*

   f  *scurries*

   g  *revolutionise*

**h** *charismatic*

**6** Explain in your own words: **[2 marks each: 4]**

   **a** *our predatory ancestry means we put up with a lot more abuse before we run.*

   **b** *positive actions reap positive consequences; negative actions incur negative consequences.*

**7** What does Monty mean when he says *'There's not a bad kid born. ... There's not a bad horse born.'*? **[2]**

**8** Quote the phrase which shows that the writer is impressed by the personality of Monty. **[1]**

**9** Quote two words or phrases which show that the writer is impressed by the achievement of Monty. **[2]**

**10** By using details from paragraphs 4 and 5, write a summary of the process Monty uses for taming a wild horse. Write a paragraph of between 50 and 70 words. **[6]**

[Total: 30 marks]

# Answers to Worksheet for Text 3

**1** Explain in your own words *He looks the part*. [1]

**His appearance is as one would expect it to be/ he is wearing the clothes of a cowboy.**

**2** Explain the meaning of *In the horse world he's a bit of a god*. [1]

**People who work with horses think he has divine powers.**

**3** Why does Monty say that no horses have read or heard about him? [2]

**He says this to make clear that the effect he has on horses can have nothing to do with his reputation.**

**4** Explain, using your own words, what the writer means by: [1 mark each: 3]

   **a** *so magical as to beggar belief*

   **The animal's inexplicable behaviour is incredible / it seems to be under a spell.**

   **b** *It's second nature to him.*

   **He can do it without having to even think about it / it comes naturally.**

   **c** *it is only a sideshow*

   **It is not the main reason for his being there / it is not his main interest.**

**5** Give another word or phrase for each of the following: [1 mark each: 8]

   **a** *techniques* – **skills / methods**

   **b** *credited with* – **given the recognition for / named as the person responsible for**

   **c** *acknowledges* – **notices / appreciates**

   **d** *collusion* – **partnership / working together**

   **e** *imitating* – **copying actions of / mimicking**

   **f** *scurries* – **moves quickly**

   **g** *revolutionise* – **completely change**

   **h** *charismatic* – **charming / fascinating**

**6** Explain in your own words: [4]

  **a** *our predatory ancestry means we put up with a lot more abuse before we run.*

  **Because we are descended from hunters we tolerate more maltreatment before escaping.**

  **b** *positive actions reap positive consequences; negative actions incur negative consequences.*

  **If you react to a situation with constructive measures the outcome will be equally constructive, and the opposite is also true, so that destructive approaches lead to destructive outcomes.**

**7** What does Monty mean when he says 'There's not a bad kid born. ... There's not a bad horse born.'? [2]

  **He means that when they first come into the world, both children and horses are potentially good, and it is only what happens to them later which makes them difficult to handle.**

**8** Quote the phrase which shows that the writer is impressed by the personality of Monty. [1]

  ***charismatic, articulate but modest***

**9** Quote two words or phrases which show that the writer is impressed by the achievement of Monty. [2]

  ***incredible; just as Monty said he would*** (allow *magic*)

**10** By using details from paragraphs 4 and 5, write a summary of the process of taming a wild horse. Write a paragraph of between 50 and 70 words. [6]

  Points to be included:
  - **Monty throws a line over the horse's back**
  - **Monty kicks up earth in the arena**
  - **Monty walks sideways towards the horse several times**
  - **Monty runs away several times when the horse turns towards him**
  - **The horse submits and follows Monty**
  - **Then a saddle is put on the horse**
  - **Finally the horse is ridden around the arena**

# Answers – Unit 3

**2** See Worksheet for Text 3 answers.

**4** The following points should be mentioned for a high Reading mark:

   **a** Wild and unridden horses willingly allow a saddle to be put on their backs and a rider to mount them; horses lose their fears and bad habits within a few minutes; I can achieve this just by speaking to them and touching them gently.

   **b** Horses are much wiser than humans; they have been around for much longer; they learn quickly; they are flight animals.

   Children are more important than horses; they put up with a lot of abuse before running away.

   Animals and children have similar needs: trust and safety and love. They are afraid of pain. Both horses and children are born potentially good, but get damaged by circumstances and the way they are treated. Both need teaching and enlightened teachers.

   **c** Success is due to many years' experience of allowing horses to teach me; a positive is always more effective than a negative approach, i.e. rewards not punishments; instead of conflict, deals should be made which involve both sides; these encourage responsibility; rewards should consist of pleasurable and memorable experiences.

   For a high Writing mark out of 5, there needs to be overall structure, sequence, clarity, and a variety of appropriate language used in the response.

**6** Text 3: style analysis:

The article has the news report features of: direct speech from interviewee, use of present tense, eye witness account, short sentences, short paragraphs. These give the effects of immediacy, the personality of the subject, the authenticity of the event, and a sense of drama.

The article has the magazine article features of: lack of sense of immediacy, the personal attitude of the reporter, the use of the first person, longer paragraphs. These give the effects of consideration, engagement and conviction and the implication is that this is a significant and ongoing topic rather than just an ephemeral event.

Text 3 moves between the two styles and perspectives, even within the same paragraph.

# Responding to reading

## Unit 4 City portraits

### Topic outline

- **Syllabus component:** Paper 1; Paper 2 questions 1 and 2; Paper 3 section 2 question 3; Paper 4 assignment 1
- **Main skills:** responding to reading; analysing effects; genre transformation
- **Secondary skills:** descriptive writing; informative writing
- **Outcome:** travel writing; guide book entry; *blog entry; *informative coursework
- **Materials:** magazine travel articles
- **Texts:** Text 4A: Krakow and Lisbon; Text 4B: Tokyo

### Lesson plan

1. Ask students to skim-read Text 4A. (5)

2. Ask students to give the meanings and effects of the ten underlined words in Text 4A. (10)

3. Elicit feedback. Discuss how effects go beyond meanings because of the connotations of words. (5)

4. Ask students, in pairs, to find and identify examples of the characteristics of travel writing in Text 4A. Collect feedback and list on board. (5)

5. Ask students to plan and write an additional section for Text 4A, of about half a page, describing interesting features of a city they know, in the same style as the entries for Krakow and Lisbon. (10)

6. Allow time for students to check and correct their responses, then collect work to assess for appropriateness of style and use of detail. (5)

7. Ask students to draw what comes to mind when they hear the name Tokyo, and choose students to draw their responses on the board. Discuss why places are linked to particular images. Now tell students to look at the illustration to Text 4B and say how this image compares with their own. (5)

8. Read Text 4B aloud to students. Ask students to recall words and suggest why they are memorable. (5)

9. Ask students to scan Text 4B and underline words evoking a sensory response, putting them under the headings of the five senses. (10)

10. Collect feedback in columns on board; ask students to explain why the choices effectively evoke the mood and atmosphere of the place. (10)

11. Write *Mosquitoes* and *Wedding* on the board, two words from Text 4B, and ask students to call out words and phrases to complete an iceberg diagram for each. (Move downwards through the layers from denotation to primary and then to secondary connotation.) (10)

12. Ask students to identify and highlight the parts of Text 4B which are the writer's opinion or reflection about Tokyo rather than fact. (5)

13. Elicit feedback and discuss the role of opinion in travel writing and guide books. (5)

### Homework task

You are Andrew Miller, the writer of Text 4B, and you have been asked to write the introduction to the Tokyo entry for a new guide book to Japan. Select from the information and observations in the airline magazine article, and adopt an appropriate style for the new audience and purpose. You should write between a side and a side and a half of average-size writing.

### Additional tasks

a  Ask students to imagine they have visited Krakow or Lisbon and feel that the impression given in Text 4A is misleading. Ask them to explain their view in a blog entry, giving reasons and providing supporting details.

b  For a coursework assignment 1, ask students to plan and draft an article called 'Portrait of a city' for a different city, using Text 4B as a model.

# Text 4A

# Poland and Portugal

### Krakow

A few days in Poland gives a perfect snapshot of eastern European history. Krakow's misty, cobbled streets are full of grand buildings, family homes acquired by the communists after the war. Our guide pointed to what is now a McDonald's and sighed – she lived in a 1970s tower block, 20 minutes' drive from the town centre. Krakow university dates from 1364 and the Copernicus hotel, close to the romantic spires of the Wawel (royal castle), once housed 14th-century students. Their modern equivalents favour kebabs and Coke; we opted for the more traditional borscht […] in what appeared to be somebody's front room, with Chopin accompaniment from a young piano player.

Beautiful, tragic Kazimierz is the city's Jewish quarter. In 1939, 70,000 Jews lived there; now there are 180. A 'Schindler tour' goes from here to Auschwitz, 60 kilometres west, but we headed to Nowa Huta, a 1950s steelworkers' suburb, the grey architecture of which matched our preconceptions perfectly.

'Krakow is the capital of souls, Warsaw the capital of administration,' Krakovians told us. Our Warsaw hotel, the Europejski (19th-century, blocky Soviet refit inside), overlooked the central square; young soldiers were on parade. We took the lift to the 30th floor of the Palace of Culture and Science, a gift from Stalin. Hardly a street survived being razed by the Nazis, but the charming Old Town was meticulously rebuilt after the war.

Light relief came in the form of a retro cabaret show and kitsch Japanese installations at the Centre for Contemporary Art, followed by a dose of colour courtesy of Bacon, Dali, Picasso and a whole roomful of Warhols at the Zacheta gallery.

For a brief glimpse of rural Poland we drove through the mountainous Beskidy region, past mysterious lakes, farmers using hand-held ploughs, and vivid yellow shrines. Finally we found Zakopane ('something hidden'), the country's top ski resort. We were the only foreigners. The two-hour bus ride back to Krakow cost just €1.20.

### Lisbon

On a weekend of torrential rain and electrical storms, few places in Lisbon offer more comfort than the Hotel Lapa Palace, perched near the brow of one of the city's seven hills in the elegant Lapa district. Sitting by a window in the hotel's restaurant Cipriani, watching the rubber trees outside silhouetted by lightning and, beyond, the choppy waters of the River Tagus sweeping out to the Atlantic, sets you wondering how this small corner of the Iberian peninsula was once the capital of the Old World.

Lisbon is trying to transform itself into the new Barcelona – a stopover for the culture cognoscenti. Over the past four years, a group of architects and designers have organised an art and design biennial in the city. A string of nightclubs and bars have sprung up in warehouses along the waterfront, […] but the city can always fall back on the charm of its faded elegance. There is simple pleasure in just strolling the streets in the old Moorish quarter of Alfama or snaking up and down its steep hills in clattering antiquated trams. Later, it is time to listen to the Portuguese equivalent of the blues in one of Lisbon's many fado houses. The most frequent themes of those melancholic songs are, appropriately, loss and longing.

Source: *Sunday Times Magazine*.

# Portrait of a city: Tokyo

*A teacher's year in the bewitching capital of Japan*

Westerners still arrive in Tokyo hoping to find an old Japan of shrines and paper houses, of shy women and inscrutable men. They leave after a week, puzzled and disappointed. Others expect a technological wonderland and find something of that in the department stores of Akihabara, but find something else too, something unexpected, resonant, mysterious.

In my first weeks in Tokyo, […] impression succeeded impression with a rapidity that made assimilation impossible. Other than knowing I was in the capital city of Japan and one of the great concentrations of humanity on the planet, I didn't really know where I was. As time passed, I seemed to be travelling away from any understanding of the place, to be more and more bewildered, as though I had wandered into a stranger's dream. Much initial effort went into trying to avoid getting lost or, having become so, into trying to find something – anything – that looked familiar. Each time I left my little apartment in the city's western suburbs I was never quite sure I would see it again. I would pause at street corners and look back at the way I had come, memorising landmarks but somehow not quite believing in them, as though that blue-tiled roof, or the rattling, pinging pachinko parlour, might have drifted away like incense smoke before I returned.

Summer, hot and humid, is not an easy season in Tokyo. The locals carry little folded cloths to mop the sweat from their faces but staying cool was a struggle. Nights were not much easier. I would lie on my little roll-out mattress, an electric fan whirring beside my head, mosquitoes flying tirelessly above. Some days the air was thick as soup. I longed to escape to the country, to the mountains or the coast, but could hardly be bothered to put on my sandals. Anyway, I was working, moving through the looping guts of the Tokyo transport system, arriving at hard-to-identify places to sing alphabet songs with pre-school children or, in the evenings, to teach English to their older brothers and sisters.

When I wasn't teaching, I was training. The world headquarters of aikido – 'the way of harmony', a martial-art cousin of judo and jujitsu – was in downtown Shinjuku, and by getting off my futon at some unlikely hour of the morning, I could get down there in time for the 8 a.m. class or, more heroically, the 6 a.m. Some of my happiest hours in Tokyo were spent in the training hall being hurled around by people who had spent 20, 30, 40 years in the art. The oldest practitioners I called the 'grey belts' as their black belts, won so long ago, had faded to a ragged pearl colour. Among them were men – and the occasional woman – in their 70s or 80s. I was terrified at first of accidentally killing one of them but soon learnt that I was the one likely to need rescuing.

On days off from teaching, pleasantly weary after my exertions on the mat, I would wander in the curling alleyways of Shinjuku revelling in the ordinary business of the people who lived and worked there: the bar owners, the housewives, schoolgirls in tartan skirts, a monk in saffron. There was a barber's shop I used to visit where the barber, wearing a surgical mask over his mouth (for his protection or mine?) would shave me – the hairy foreigner – with a thoroughness that included scraping his razor over my forehead, clipping my nasal hairs and plucking the hairs from my ears with tweezers. Hot flannels were laid over my face, then unguents out of curious bell jars were rubbed vigorously into my skin while the man's daughter used her cupped hands to massage my shoulders. It was not an expensive indulgence – Japan can be surprisingly good value …

September means typhoons, and a certain historic nervousness. Days of warm swirling rain, inescapable rain. Everything rots. Then, quite suddenly, the fug of summer is blown away by the first cool breezes of the autumn. As the mornings turned chilly, I would buy a can of hot sweet coffee from the vending machines by my local station, sipping it between the swaying and dozing salarymen on the Toei-Shinjuku line.

When did the snow come? December? February? I cannot quite remember, but have a vivid recollection of walking home one afternoon through the grounds of the Shinto shrine in Motoyawata and seeing a winter wedding, the bride in her silken hood, the groom sombre in his hakama. To keep off the snow, the wedding party carried umbrellas of lacquered paper. The couple, shy and serious, paused for photos then, on wooden sandals, everyone tottered off, while behind them, on the frozen water of the purification trough, the snow continued its soft descent. I could have stayed forever (I almost did), feeding on the city's casual poetry – a creature lost in translation, but perfectly content to be so.

Source: Andrew Miller, *High Life Magazine*, British Airways, September 2008.

# Answers – Unit 4

**2**   Text 4A: meanings and effects:

preconceptions – means expectations with the force of prejudgements and even prejudices; these often turn out to be false, but were accurate in this case

blocky – this word does not exist, but suggests squares and angles and concrete (the 'breeze blocks' beloved of cheap builders) and by extension greyness, lack of imagination or individuality, and the opposite of luxury and comfort

razed – destroyed to the ground, with nothing left standing, can only be critical of those who caused the destruction, even when it is being used as a purely objective descriptive word

meticulously – means thoroughly, and here shows approval for the way in which the damage was faithfully restored to its original splendour

retro – is really a prefix meaning looking backwards; in some contexts this would have negative connotations, but here it is a fashionable concept and desirable commodity

kitsch – of German origin, this adjective is usually a criticism of something which appeals to popular and undiscriminating taste, but here it is being used as a neutral trendy term

dose – because this word is associated with medicine and illness, its effect is measured and subdued, negating the idea of colour – unlike the synonym *dash*, which would imply abandon, flair and brightness

perched – meaning balanced on an edge, this metaphorical word brings a little poetic force to the description by the implied comparison of the hotel with a bird

biennial – this word meaning every two years (not to be confused with *biannual* which means twice a year) gives concision to the factual style; the noun – *exhibition* or *event* – is only implied

melancholic – although the meaning is generally a negative one – explained in the same line as evocative of *loss and longing* – it is here associated with romance and feeling so connotes a more positive mood, and one linked to nostalgia, another ambivalent feeling

**4**   Text 4A: travel writing style:

Although superficially a purely informative genre of writing, there is usually also a poetic/figurative element of language to make the place seductive – or at least to convince the reader that the writer did actually visit the place – even though there is no reason why the writer needs to persuade readers to visit these places, there being no financial incentive involved.

The most recognisable features of travel writing are:

references to the permanent cultural and landscape features which can be visited; appositional phrases and avoidance of *and* for concision; alternatives to regular word order to avoid monotony; references to food, restaurants; use of sounds, and other senses; use of words in the local language; mixing facts with inferences, opinions and personal reponses; the use of the first person and *you*; multiple adjectival usage; use of imagery and poetic language (e.g. alliteration) to evoke atmosphere, but not so much that it ceases to be informative and becomes descriptive writing; the metaphors tend to be unoriginal (e.g. *perched* and *snaking*).

**10** Text 4B: sensory description:

**Sight** – *blue-tiled roof; the mountains or the coast; the looping guts of the Tokyo transport system; hurled around; faded to a ragged pearl colour; curling alleyways; schoolgirls in tartan skirts, a monk in saffron; wearing a surgical mask over his mouth; the hairy foreigner; curious bell jars; seeing a winter wedding; umbrellas of lacquered paper; the snow continued its soft descent*

**Sound** – *rattling, pinging pachinko parlour; an electric fan whirring, mosquitoes flying; sing alphabet songs; typhoons; wooden sandals*

**Smell** – *like incense smoke; unguents*

**Taste** – *the air was thick as soup; hot sweet coffee*

**Touch** – *hot and humid; folded cloths to mop the sweat from their faces; scraping his razor over my forehead; plucking the hairs; Hot flannels; rubbed vigorously into my skin; massage my shoulders; warm swirling rain; cool breezes; chilly*

Many of the above imply more than one sense, e.g. *drifted away like incense smoke* (also sight), *an electric fan whirring* (also touch), *the air was thick as soup* (also touch), *hurled around* (also touch) and *saffron* (also taste). The verb *rots* conjures up both sight and smell, and *fug* fuses several senses, as do *snow* and *rain* and *frozen*.

This is called synaesthesia and is a poetic device which can also be used in descriptive writing generally to strengthen the sensuous effect of words and images. What makes the description of this text particularly striking is that it contains many touch images, whereas description tends to concentrate on sight and sound rather than the more intimate, and therefore more evocative, other three senses.

Note also how sound is conveyed through the use of alliteration which is also onomatopoeic (e.g. *pinging pachinko parlour; snow continued its soft descent*).

**11** Text 4B: example of iceberg diagrams for *mosquitoes* and *wedding*:

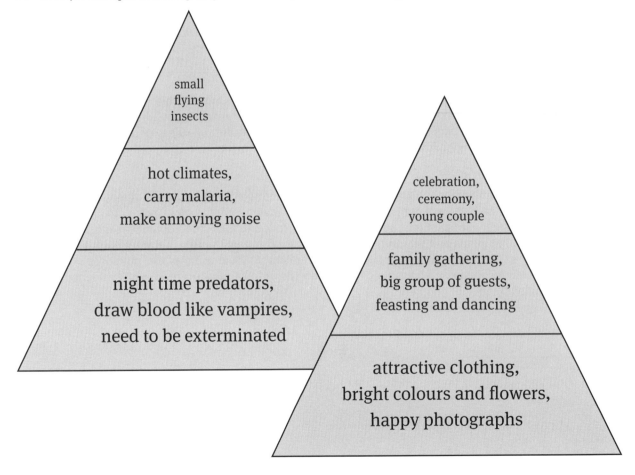

**12** Text 4B: opinions and inferences:

old Japan has gone; Japan not just about new technology but something less tangible; Tokyo is a hard place to get to know; Tokyo is dreamlike; elderly experts in aikido are amazing and make formidable opponents; the greatest pleasure is to go among ordinary people; a visit to the barber is an intense and enjoyable physical experience; the winter wedding was visually striking and memorable; Tokyo is a poetic place.

**13** Transforming travel writing to guide book entry:

All the factual material and pure description should be included in the guide book adaptation (e.g. references to climate). The first person and references to his job and hobbies should be removed completely and the persona should become *a visitor* or *you*. A small and carefully selected number of reflections and experiences may be included, but not those which are purely personal and would not have universal application, or those which were seen by chance and would not be still there for a future visitor (e.g. the wedding). The visit to the barber for a shave and massage should not be included in its present form, but can be part of a description of the kinds of things to be found or experienced in the alleyways. The imagery and poetic language of the passage needs to be paraphrased and toned down to make it more appropriate for an informative piece of writing. There should still be plenty of description and evocation of atmosphere, but it needs to be in the student's own words. They may infer and develop points and ideas used in the original text, provided that they do not stray too far from it.

# Stylistic effects

## Unit 5 Memorable characters

**Topic outline**

- **Syllabus component:** Paper 2 question 2; Paper 3 section 2 questions 3 and 4
- **Main skills:** identifying writers' effects
- **Secondary skills:** narrative devices; use of dialogue; punctuation revision
- **Outcome:** analysis of writers' effects; *descriptive writing
- **Materials:** autobiographical passages
- **Texts:** Text 5A: My first drive; Text 5B: The Rose-beetle Man

## Lesson plan

1  Assign roles from Text 5A (narrator, five children, older sister and mother) and read as drama. (5)

2  When do we use commas? Elicit the rules for comma usage and list on board (i.e. to separate clauses, for parenthesis, to separate items in lists). Ask students to find examples of each usage in Text 5A. (5)

3  When do we use hyphens? Ask students to circle all the hyphens in Text 5A and formulate a rule for their usage (i.e. to connect two words acting as one and which cannot exist meaningfully alone). Elicit rules. (5)

4  How do we punctuate dialogue? Ask students, in pairs, to study the punctuation of the dialogue in Text 5A and formulate rules. Elicit rules and write on board. (5)

5  Ask students to re-read Text 5A and in pairs to identify and list the content and style features of narrative writing. (10)

6  Collect features on board and explain reason for and effect of each. (10)

7  Ask students, in pairs, to identify how the sense of drama has been created in Text 5A (i.e. conflict, tension and suspense). Invite responses including examples. (5)

8  How might the dialogue continue? Elicit suggestions for a further exchange in Text 5A and agree on the most convincing. (5)

9  Ask students to offer adjectives of their own to describe the character of the 'ancient sister', supported by evidence from Text 5A referring to her speech, appearance and actions. (5)

10  Ask students to read Text 5B and draw the Rose-beetle Man. (5)

11  Tell the students to imagine a conversation between the young boy and the Rose-beetle Man. Ask them to write a short dialogue of three questions or answers each, set out according to the punctuation rules on the board and avoiding the use of *said*. (10)

12  Ask students to swap their dialogues and correct each other's punctuation. Invite pairs to read out their dialogues. (5)

13  Ask students to underline words and phrases in Text 5B (at least ten) which convey the appearance of the Rose-beetle Man. (5)

14  Now ask them to transfer their underlined quotations to a list and to write an explanation for each one of the effect it conveys and how it does so. (10)

### Homework task

Using your underlined choices, write a full response of about a page to the question: How has the writer given the impression that the Rose-beetle Man is a) weird and fascinating, and b) deserving of our sympathy? Answer the question in two parts. Explain why each choice is effective in evoking a reader response.

### Additional task

Ask students to write a piece of description entitled 'A memorable character'. They should give the character a context/surroundings, and describe in close detail their appearance and manner. They could also include examples of the way they talk.

**Text 5A**

# My first drive

The weather was exceptionally mild that Christmas holiday and one amazing morning our whole family got ready to go for our first drive in the first motor-car we had ever owned. The driver was to be that 12-years-older-than-me-half-sister, who was now aged 21. She had received two full half-hour lessons in driving from the man who delivered the car, and this was considered quite sufficient. As we all climbed into the car, our excitement was so intense we could hardly bear it.

'How fast will it go?' we cried out. 'Will it do 80 kilometres an hour?'

'It'll do 90!' the ancient sister answered. Her tone was so confident it should have scared us to death, but it didn't. 'We shall probably go faster than that,' the sister announced, pulling on her driving-gloves and tying her scarf.

The canvas hood had been folded back because of the mild weather. My mother, half-brother, three sisters and I were all quivering with fear and joy as the driver let out the clutch and the great, long, black automobile leapt into motion.

'Are you sure you know what to do?' we shouted. 'Do you know where the brakes are?'

'Be quiet!' snapped the ancient sister. 'I've got to concentrate!'

Down the drive we went, and out into the village, with the driver pressing the rubber bulb of the horn every time we passed a human being. Soon we were entering a countryside of green fields and high hedges with not a soul in sight.

'You didn't think I could do it, did you?' cried the ancient sister, turning round and grinning at us all.

'Now you keep your eyes on the road,' my mother said nervously.

'Go faster!' we shouted. 'Put your foot down!'

Spurred on by our shouts, the ancient sister began to increase the speed. The engine roared and the body vibrated. The driver was clutching the steering-wheel as though it were the hair of a drowning man, and we all watched the speedometer needle creeping up. We were probably doing about 50 kilometres an hour when we came suddenly to a sharpish bend in the road. The ancient sister, never having been faced with a situation like this before, shouted 'Help!' and slammed on the brakes and swung the wheel wildly. The rear wheels locked and went into a fierce sideways skid, and then, with a marvellous crunch of mudguards and metal, we went crashing into the hedge. The front passengers all shot through the front windscreen and the back passengers all shot through the back windscreen. Glass flew in all directions, and so did we. But miraculously nobody was hurt very much, except me. My nose had been cut almost clean off my face and now it was hanging on by a single small thread of skin. My mother disentangled herself from the wreckage and grabbed a handkerchief from her purse. She clapped the dangling nose back into place and held it there.

Not a cottage or a person was in sight, let alone a telephone. Some kind of bird started twittering in a tree farther down the road, otherwise all was silent.

**Adapted from *Boy* by Roald Dahl, Penguin, 1986.**

# Text 5B

# The Rose-beetle Man

*The extract describes the meeting on the Greek island of Corfu between a young boy and an itinerant seller of beetles tied to ribbons.*

Perhaps one of the most weird and fascinating characters I met during my travels was the Rose-beetle Man. He had a fairy-tale air about him that was impossible to resist, and I used to look forward eagerly to my infrequent meetings with him. I first saw him on a high, lonely road leading to one of the remote mountain villages. I could hear him long before I could see him, for he was playing a rippling tune on a shepherd's pipe, breaking off now and then to sing a few words in a curious, nasal voice. As he rounded the corner both my dog and I stopped and stared at him in amazement.

He had a sharp, fox-like face with large slanting eyes of such a dark brown that they appeared black. They had a weird, vacant-look about them, and a sort of bloom such as one finds on a plum, a pearly covering almost like a cataract. He was short and slight, with a thinness about his wrists […] that argued a lack of food. His dress was fantastic, and on his head was a shapeless hat with a very wide, floppy brim. It had once been bottle-green, but was now speckled and smeared with dust, wine-stains and cigarette-burns. In the band were stuck a fluttering forest of feathers. […] His shirt was worn and frayed, grey with sweat, and round the neck dangled an enormous cravat of the most startling blue satin. His coat was dark and shapeless, with patches of different hues here and there; on the sleeve a bit of white cloth with a design of rosebuds; on the shoulder a triangular patch of red and white spots. The pockets of this garment bulged, the contents spilling out, […] including a riot of handkerchiefs. His trousers, patched like his coat, drooped over a pair of scarlet leather shoes with upturned toes decorated with large black-and-white pompons.

**Source:** *My Family and Other Animals* **by Gerald Durrell, Penguin, 1959.**

# Answers – Unit 5

**4** Rules for the punctuation of dialogue:
- start a new line for a change of speaker
- include some form of punctuation before closing inverted commas
- use a small letter for the beginning of the word which continues the sentence after the speech closes, even if the final speech punctuation is a question or exclamation mark (and it cannot be a full stop)
- use a comma to introduce speech within a sentence before opening inverted commas

*Note:* Although printed text uses single inverted commas for speech, in handwriting double are used, to distinguish speech from ironic usage or jargon.

**6** Text 5A: features of narrative:

Although Text 5A is autobiographical, it has the same features as fictional narrative: two or three main characters (more becomes confusing); dialogue (for dramatic effect, variety, and to allow voices to reveal character); changes of pace (to build up tension or convey panic); figurative language (similes and metaphors create images to clarify meaning); multiple adjectival usage (to give maximum detail of setting or character); time references (to create apprehension and expectation); references to season and weather and time of day (to enable reader to picture the scene).

**7** How Text 5A has been made dramatic:

Because the weather was *exceptionally mild* and the morning was *amazing* we are expecting something extraordinary to happen, and the phrase *it should have scared us to death* foreshadows that it will not be a good thing. The children are *quivering with fear and joy* which are strong emotions and create a heightened mood. Calling his 21-year-old sister *ancient* prepares us for her being unsatisfactory or a figure of fun. Emphasis is placed on the car by describing it as *the great, long, black automobile*, and the fact that it is personified as having *leapt into motion* signifies that something will happen because of the car, which makes us expect there to be an accident. Because the sister *snapped* when they asked her to go faster, we know that she is stressed and this means that she may make a mistake. The mother is behaving *nervously* which reveals she is afraid. The simile *as if it were the hair of a drowning man* is an unpleasant image to introduce the idea of life-threatening danger. When the sister shouts *Help!* we realise that the car is out of control at high speed and so a collision is inevitable, since she is unable to do anything to stop it, as is shown by the word *wildly*. The verb *slammed* is violent and calls attention to the emergency situation. The alliterative phrase *marvellous crunch of mudguards and metal* strongly emphasises the severity of the crash, as in this case *marvellous* means amazing, like something that might happen in a film. *Glass flew in all directions* is an exaggeration for dramatic effect, but we associate even a small amount of broken glass with injury. That his nose is now only attached by a *single small thread of skin* emphasises how nearly it has come off completely, and how it may still do so.

The syntax in the passage is exaggerated or extreme, and the number of short questions and exclamations give an overall effect of tension and drama to the events. There is a lot of noise to lead up to the climax and provide a contrast to the sudden silence, which shows that something awful has now happened and they don't know what to do about it.

**9** Text 5A: 'ancient sister' description:

Adjectives to describe her are over-confident (*considered quite sufficient*, *We shall probably go faster than that*); showing off (*It'll do 90!*, *pressing the rubber bulb of the horn*); bad-tempered (*Be quiet!*); self-satisfied (*grinning*); flustered (*Help!*).

**Homework task:** (to be marked out of 10)

*How has the writer given the impression that the Rose-beetle Man is a) weird and fascinating, and b) deserving of our sympathy?*

**a** He is made to seem weird and fascinating, and *impossible to resist*, because the reference to *fairy-tale* suggests that he has magic powers. His *curious, nasal voice* when he sings makes him sound different from other people, and his eyes are *such a dark brown* that they were more *fox-like* than human. Describing his clothing as *fantastic* again connect him to fairy tales. He does not just have one feather in his hat, but a *fluttering forest* of them, which stresses how many of them there were, and that they were in constant movement. Likewise, *a riot of handkerchiefs* suggests not only quantity but also noise and violent movement. He is wearing a mixture of *different hues* which are so many and so bright and the effect so *startling* that even the dog *stopped in amazement*, as he had never seem any human like this before. The exact detail of *a triangular patch of red and white spots* creates a bizarre visual effect of contrasting colours and shapes. The main colour is bright red, which reminds us of the costume of a clown. The overall effect is that everything about the figure is unusual and forms a bizarre spectacle, which the onlooker's gaze becomes fixed on because of the surprise combinations of colour and the constant movement.

**b** The reader feels sympathy for him because the *pearly covering* on his eyes suggests he cannot see properly, and the *thinness about the wrists* shows he does not get enough to eat. Because his clothes are *speckled and smeared with dust* we know he only has one set of clothes, which he has to patch. The state of his *worn and frayed* clothing suggests that he has no one to look after him or care about him, but that he is unable to look after himself and wash his clothes. Because his cravat is of *blue satin*, which is a material associated with luxury, we get the impression that previously he was better off and better dressed than he is now. The fact that his hat is *floppy*, his trousers *drooped*, and his shoes have *upturned toes* and a *pompon* contribute to a total picture of a clown whose clothes are all too big for him. This means that we think of him as someone who is brightly and comically dressed, yet who may be sad.

# Stylistic effects

## Unit 6 Just walking

### Topic outline

- **Syllabus component:** Paper 2 question 2; Paper 3 section 2 question 4
- **Main skills:** identifying writers' effects; making inferences
- **Secondary skills:** narrative structure; using imagery; identifying irony
- **Outcome:** analysis of writers' effects; character's diary; *narrative composition
- **Materials:** futuristic short story
- **Text:** Text 6: The pedestrian

## Lesson plan

1  Assign the roles of narrator, character and police car and read Text 6 aloud in three voices. (5)

2  What can we tell about the writer's attitude? Ask students to make inferences, giving evidence to support them, from Text 6 about: a) the writer's attitude to television, b) his attitude to the police, c) his attitude to life in 2053, d) what is likely to happen to Leonard Mead. (10)

3  Ask students to first underline all the words or phrases in paragraphs 1, 2 and 3 which describe the environment and atmosphere, and then to write a sentence which gives an overview of the combined overall effect of their choices. (5)

4  Read out the list of words while students check against their own. Choose students to read out their statements of overall effect. (5)

5  Write on the board the following first halves of similes. Ask students to write completions which convey a sinister urban atmosphere:

   a  The streets were so empty it was as if ...
   b  The air was as cold as ...
   c  The concrete apartment blocks were like ...
   d  The greyness of everything gave the impression that ...
   e  The silence reminded them of ... (10)

6  Invite responses and judge them. (5)

7  Ask students, in pairs, to identify the different stages in the story. (5)

8  Invite answers and list stages on board. Discuss how each change adds tension. (5)

9  Ask students to write an opening paragraph to a story set in a city in the future, using the same devices of giving location, season, weather, time of day, and using mood images. (10)

10  Tell students, in pairs, to swap paragraphs and comment on each other's. Would they wish to read further in the story? Why, or why not? (5)

11  Ask students, in small groups, to script and practise the dialogue which might take place in the Psychiatric Center for Research on Regressive Tendencies after Leonard's arrival there, and which would give a new ending to the story. (15)

12  Ask the students to perform their sketches. Choose the best and give reasons. (10)

### Homework tasks

How has the writer of 'The pedestrian' made the story ironic? Identify and explain the effect of all the different ways in which irony has been used in the text.

### Additional tasks

a  Ask students to write Leonard Mead's final diary entry, using material from the story and revealing what has happened to him in the psychiatric centre, and what he thinks is going to happen to him next.

b  Ask students to use the stages listed in task 8 to write their own short story called 'The pedestrian', about an event which happens to someone, somewhere, who is out walking.

© Cambridge University Press 2010

# The pedestrian
By Ray Bradbury

To enter out into that silence that was the city at eight o'clock of a misty evening in November, to put your feet upon that buckling concrete walk, to step over grassy seams and make your way, hands in pockets, through the silences, that was what Mr Leonard Mead most dearly loved to do. He would stand upon the corner of an intersection and peer down long moonlit avenues of sidewalk in four directions, deciding which way to go, but it really made no difference; he was alone in this world of 2053 A.D., or as good as alone, and with a final decision made, a path selected, he would stride off, sending patterns of frosty air before him like the smoke of a cigar.

Sometimes he would walk for hours and miles and return only at midnight to his house. And on his way he would see the cottages and homes with their dark windows, and it was not unequal to walking through a graveyard where only the faintest glimmers of firefly light appeared in flickers behind the windows. Sudden gray phantoms seemed to manifest upon inner room walls where a curtain was still undrawn against the night, or there were whisperings and murmurs where a window in a tomb-like building was still open.

Mr Leonard Mead would pause, cock his head, listen, look, and march on, his feet making no noise on the lumpy walk. For long ago he had wisely changed to sneakers when strolling at night, because the dogs in intermittent squads would parallel his journey with barkings if he wore hard heels, and lights might click on and faces appear and an entire street be startled by the passing of a lone figure, himself, in the early November evening.

On this particular evening he began his journey in a westerly direction, toward the hidden sea. There was a good crystal frost in the air; it cut the nose and made the lungs blaze like a Christmas tree inside; you could feel the cold light going on and off, all the branches filled with invisible snow. He listened to the faint push of his soft shoes through autumn leaves with satisfaction, and whistled a cold quiet whistle between his teeth, occasionally picking up a leaf as he passed, examining its skeletal pattern in the infrequent lamplights as he went on, smelling its rusty smell.

'Hello, in there,' he whispered to every house on every side as he moved. 'What's up tonight on Channel 4, Channel 7, Channel 9? Where are the cowboys rushing, and do I see the United States Cavalry over the next hill to the rescue?'

The street was silent and long and empty, with only his shadow moving like the shadow of a hawk in mid-country. If he closed his eyes and stood very still, frozen, he could imagine himself upon the center of a plain, a wintry, windless Arizona desert with no house in a thousand miles, and only dry river beds, the street, for company.

'What is it now?' he asked the houses, noticing his wrist watch. 'Eight-thirty P.M.? Time for a dozen assorted murders? A quiz? A revue? A comedian falling off the stage?'

Was that a murmur of laughter from within a moon-white house? He hesitated, but went on when nothing more happened. He stumbled over a particularly uneven section of sidewalk. The cement was vanishing under flowers and grass. In ten years of walking by night or day, for thousands of miles, he had never met another person walking, not one in all that time.

He came to a cloverleaf intersection which stood silent where two main highways crossed the town. During the day it was a thunderous surge of cars, the gas stations open, a great insect rustling and a ceaseless jockeying for position as the scarab-beetles, a faint incense puttering from their exhausts, skimmed homeward to the far directions. But now these highways, too, were like streams in a dry season, all stone and bed and moon radiance.

He turned back on a side street, circling around toward his home. He was within a block of his destination when the lone car turned a corner quite suddenly and flashed a fierce white cone of light upon him. He stood entranced, not unlike a night moth, stunned by the illumination, and then drawn toward it.

A metallic voice called to him:

'Stand still. Stay where you are! Don't move!'

He halted.

'Put up your hands!'

'But–' he said.

'Your hands up! Or we'll shoot!'

The police, of course, but what a rare, incredible thing; in a city of three million, there was only one police car left, wasn't that correct? Ever since a year ago, 2052, the election year, the force had been cut down from three cars to one. Crime was ebbing; there was no need now for the police, save for this one lone car wandering and wandering the empty streets.

'Your name?' said the police car in a metallic whisper. He couldn't see the men in it for the bright light in his eyes.

'Leonard Mead,' he said.

'Speak up!'

'Leonard Mead!'

'Business or profession?'

'I guess you'd call me a writer.'

'No profession,' said the police car, as if talking to itself. The light held him fixed, like a museum specimen, needle thrust through chest.

'You might say that,' said Mr Mead.

He hadn't written in years. Magazines and books didn't sell anymore. Everything went on in the tomb-like houses at night now, he thought, continuing his fancy. The tombs, ill-lit by television light, where the people sat like the dead, the gray or multi-colored lights touching their faces, but never really touching them.

'No profession,' said the phonograph voice, hissing. 'What are you doing out?'

'Walking,' said Leonard Mead.

'Walking!'

'Just walking,' he said simply, but his face felt cold.

'Walking, just walking, walking?'

'Yes, sir.'

'Walking where? For what?'

'Walking for air. Walking to see.'

'Your address!'

'Eleven South Saint James Street.'

'And there is air in your house, you have an air conditioner, Mr Mead?'

'Yes.'

'And you have a viewing screen in your house to see with?'

'No.'

'No?' There was a crackling quiet that in itself was an accusation.

'Are you married, Mr Mead?'

'No.'

'Not married,' said the police voice behind the fiery beam. The moon was high and clear among the stars and the houses were gray and silent.

'Nobody wanted me,' said Leonard Mead with a smile.

'Don't speak unless you're spoken to!'

Leonard Mead waited in the cold night.

'Just walking, Mr Mead?'

'Yes.'

'But you haven't explained for what purpose.'

'I explained; for air, and to see, and just to walk.'

'Have you done this often?'

'Every night for years.'

The police car sat in the center of the street with its radio throat faintly humming.

'Well, Mr Mead,' it said.

'Is that all?' he asked politely.

'Yes,' said the voice. 'Here.' There was a sigh, a pop. The back door of the police car sprang wide. 'Get in.'

'Wait a minute, I haven't done anything!'

'Get in.'

'I protest!'

'Mr Mead.'

He walked like a man suddenly drunk. As he passed the front window of the car he looked in. As he had expected, there was no one in the front seat, no one in the car at all.

'Get in.'

He put his hand to the door and peered into the back seat, which was a little cell, a little black jail with bars. It smelled of riveted steel. It smelled of harsh antiseptic; it smelled too clean and hard and metallic. There was nothing soft there.

'Now if you had a wife to give you an alibi,' said the iron voice. 'But–'

'Where are you taking me?'

The car hesitated, or rather gave a faint whirring click, as if information, somewhere, was dropping card by punch-slotted card under electric eyes. 'To the Psychiatric Center for Research on Regressive Tendencies.'

He got in. The door shut with a soft thud. The police car rolled through the night avenues, flashing its dim lights ahead.

They passed one house on one street a moment later, one house in an entire city of houses that were dark, but this one particular house had all of its electric lights brightly lit, every window a loud yellow illumination, square and warm in the cool darkness.

'That's my house,' said Leonard Mead.

No one answered him.

The car moved down the empty riverbed streets and off away, leaving the empty streets with the empty sidewalks, and no sound and no motion all the rest of the chill November night.

**Source:** 'The pedestrian' by Ray Bradbury, in *The Golden Apples of the Sun*, Avon Books, 2008.

**Note:** American spelling is used throughout this text.

# Answers – Unit 6

**2** Text 6: inferences:

   **a** We can infer that the writer of the story (as well as the persona) does not approve of mindless viewing of whatever happens to be on TV. We can infer this because the hostile police car does approve of 'viewing screens' and so the reader is positioned to disagree with it. Leonard refers to the trivial, valueless programmes which everyone but himself watches in their dim tomb-like houses, and which keep everyone captive in the evenings so that the city is silent and dead. There isn't even any crime any more because that requires initiative and non-comformity, and these qualities have died out because of the mind-numbing nature of television.

   **b** The police are presented as unreasonable and tyrannical, since they arrest Leonard unnecessarily and are suspicious of all the things which make him different and interesting. Crime has been eradicated but at the expense of deadening the human spirit. He is interrogated in staccato questions and exclamations which are threatening and make the reader realise he will not be given a fair hearing when he arrives at the detention centre he is being taken to.

   **c** Life in the cities of the future will be unattractive. Machines will rule by day and by night, and there will be nothing to enjoy looking at, nothing creative being produced, and nothing soft to the touch or brightly lit: there will be total sensory deprivation. People will not go out or socialise but will sit in their concrete boxes every evening watching endless, pointless TV. Packs of dogs will roam the streets at night. There will be no place for individuals and anyone who doesn't conform will be regarded as a threat and removed from society. Everyone is expected to get married and no-one lives alone.

   **d** Leonard stumbles and this indicates he is not going to survive. He is a pedestrian in a world which does not allow walking. The simile *not unlike a night moth, stunned by the illumination, and then drawn toward it* prefigures that he will be destroyed because of his preference for freedom, air and light. References to tombs, graveyards and the impaling of insects all imply that Leonard is going to die, and that he is an extinct species, *like a museum specimen, needle thrust through chest*. His association with soft and bright means that he cannot survive against the stronger elements of metallic hardness and universal greyness.

**3** Text 6: phrases conveying sense of environment and atmosphere:

The words *silence*, *misty*, *November*, *frosty*, *dark*, *graveyard*, *gray phantoms*, *tomb-like*, *squads*, *lone*, *desert*, *dry* convey an overall effect of an environment which is colourless, empty and silent. The atmosphere is barren and lifeless because it lacks light and warmth. This imagery links with the cold, hard, metallic words used later in the story, and contrasts with Leonard's bright yellow and warm house. It is stressed that Leonard, the only human in the story, is alone whereas his enemies are plural, in *squads*, which conveys the chilling message that he has no chance of defeating them. They are as cold, hard and inhuman as the technology and the environment.

**7** Text 6: stages in the story:

1 General scene-setting which moves into a particular evening creates expectation that something unpleasant/significant is going to happen on this occasion

2 He is nearly home when he is caught – irony of being almost safe before the danger appears

3 Introduction of another 'character' – dialogue is in the form of an interrogation, and the harsh voice and unreasonable questions and responses make it clear that there is a serious threat

4 He is physically trapped and then removed – he is no longer able to act freely and is being taken somewhere frightening

5 'Cliff-hanger' device leaves the story open-ended to make reader infer what will happen next – doom-laden last sentence recaps the previous negative imagery

# Stylistic effects

## Unit 7 Dislocation

### Topic outline

- **Syllabus component:** Paper 2 question 2; Paper 3 section 2 question 3
- **Main skills:** identifying and explaining writers' effects
- **Secondary skills:** vocabulary building; descriptive writing
- **Outcome:** analysis of effects; descriptive composition
- **Materials:** novel and short story extracts; Worksheet for Text 7A: The island; Worksheet for Text 7B: The causeway
- **Texts:** Text 7A: The island; Text 7B: The causeway; Text 7C: The river

### Lesson plan

1 Tell students they are going to study three passages about people who feel out of place in their new and alien surroundings. Have they ever experienced this feeling themselves? Ask for examples. Elicit ideas on how this effect may be achieved by writers, with examples. (10)

2 Ask students to brainstorm ideas associated with being stranded on a desert island. Collect them on the board and discuss why islands have these particular associations. (5)

3 Ask students, in pairs, to complete the gap-fill exercise on Worksheet for Text 7A, taking careful note of parts of speech. (10)

4 Invite and evaluate suggestions for each of the ten gaps. Then ask students to read the original complete version of Text 7A and to underline and comment on the original words. (10)

5 Ask students, in pairs, to select words to complete the gap-fill exercise on Worksheet for Text 7B after discussing each of the three possible choices. (10)

6 Read out the original ten words used in Text 7B. Give students the chance to argue that their choices are more in keeping with the overall effect. (5)

7 Ask students what they would notice and feel if they were travelling up the Amazon River, deeper and deeper into tropical jungle. (5)

8 Read Text 7C while students listen. Which words or phrases can they remember? Write these on the board. (5)

9 Invite reasons why those particular words and phrases stood out from the passage and what effect they convey. (5)

10 Ask students to read Text 7C, comparing the underlined words and phrases with the ones on the board to see how many are the same. (5)

11 Ask students, in pairs, to write explanations of the meanings and effects of the underlined words or phrases. (10)

12 Ask students to read out their responses and discuss them as a class. (10)

### Homework task

Choose either Text 7A or Text 7B and write a response to the question: How does the passage create the effects of isolation and threat caused by natural elements?

### Additional tasks

a Set a piece of descriptive writing, of about a side, with the title of either 'The Island' or 'The River'.

b Ask students to choose a passage in a book which describes a place with a strong atmosphere, and to read it next lesson to the class.

# Text 7A

# The island

Here, on the other side of the island, the view was utterly different. The filmy enchantments of mirage could not endure the cold ocean water, and the horizon was hard, clipped blue. Ralph wandered down to the rocks. Down here, almost on a level with the sea, you could follow with your eye the ceaseless, bulging passage of the deep sea waves. They were miles wide, apparently not breakers or the banked ridges of shallow water. They travelled the length of the island with an air of disregarding it and being set on other business; they were less a progress than a momentous rise and fall of the whole ocean. Now the sea would suck down, making cascades and waterfalls of retreating water, would sink past the rocks and plaster down the seaweed like shining hair: then pausing, gather and rise with a roar, irresistibly swelling over point and outcrop, climbing the little cliff, sending at last an arm of surf up a gully to end a yard or so from him in fingers of spray.

Wave after wave, Ralph followed the rise and fall until something of the remoteness of the sea numbed his brain. Then gradually the almost infinite size of this water forced itself on his attention. This was the divider, the barrier. On the other size of the island, swathed at midday with mirage, defended by the shield of the quiet lagoon, one might dream of rescue; but here, faced by the brute obtuseness of the ocean, the miles of division, one was clamped down, one was helpless, one was condemned, one was …

**Source:** *Lord of the Flies* **by William Golding, Faber, 2002.**

**Text 7B**

# The causeway

On the causeway path it was still quite dry underfoot but to my left I saw that the water had begun to seep nearer, quite silent now, quite slow. I wondered how deeply the path went under water when the tide was at its height. But on a still night such as this, there was plenty of time to cross in safety, though the distance was greater, now I was traversing it on foot, than it had seemed when we trotted over in Keckwick's pony cart, and the end of the causeway path seemed to be receding into the greyness ahead. I had never been quite so alone, nor felt quite so small and insignificant in a vast landscape before, and I fell into a brooding, philosophical frame of mind, struck by the absolute indifference of water and sky to my presence.

Some minutes later, I could not tell how many, I came out of my reverie, to realize that I could no longer see very far in front of me, and when I turned around I was startled to find that Eel Marsh House, too, was invisible, not because the darkness of evening had fallen, but because of a thick, damp sea-mist that had come rolling over the marshes and enveloped everything, myself, the house behind me, the end of the causeway path and the countryside ahead. It was a mist like a damp, clinging cobwebby thing, fine and yet impenetrable... I felt confused, teased by it, as though it were made up of millions of live fingers that crept over me, hung onto me and then shifted away again. Above all, it was the suddenness of it that had so unnerved and disorientated me.

**Source:** *The Woman in Black* by Susan Hill, Vintage, 1998.

# Text 7C

# The river

Towards the evening of the second day we judged ourselves about eight miles from Kurtz's station. I wanted to push on; but the manager looked grave, and told me the navigation up there was so dangerous that it would be advisable, the sun being very low already, to wait where we were till next morning. Moreover, he pointed out that if the warning to approach cautiously were to be followed, we must approach in daylight – not at dusk, or in the dark. This was sensible enough. Eight miles meant nearly three hours' steaming for us, and I could also see suspicious ripples at the upper end of the reach. Nevertheless, I was annoyed beyond expression at the delay, and most unreasonably too, since one night more could not matter much after so many months. As we had plenty of wood, and caution was the word, I brought up in the middle of the stream. The reach was narrow, straight, with high sides like a railway cutting. The dusk came gliding into it long before the sun had set. The current ran smooth and swift, but a dumb immobility sat on the banks. The living trees, lashed together by the creepers and every living bush of the undergrowth, might have been changed into stone, even to the slenderest twig, to the lightest leaf. It was not sleep – it seemed unnatural, like a state of trance. Not the faintest sound of any kind could be heard. You looked on amazed, and began to suspect yourself of being deaf – then the night came suddenly, and struck you blind as well. About three in the morning some large fish leaped, and the loud splash made me jump as though a gun had been fired. When the sun rose there was a white fog, very warm and clammy, and more blinding than the night. It did not shift or drive; it was just there, standing all round you like something solid. At eight or nine, perhaps, it lifted as a shutter lifts. We had a glimpse of the towering multitude of trees, of the immense matted jungle, with the blazing little ball of the sun hanging over it – all perfectly still – and then the white shutter came down again, smoothly, as if sliding in greased grooves. I ordered the chain, which we had begun to heave in, to be paid out again. Before it stopped running with a muffled rattle, a cry, a very loud cry, as of infinite desolation, soared slowly in the opaque air.

Source: *The Heart of Darkness* by Joseph Conrad.

# Worksheet for Text 7A: The island

Fill each blank with one word.

Here, on the other side of the island, the view was utterly different. The (1) _____ enchantments of mirage could not endure the cold ocean water, and the horizon was hard, (2) _____ blue. Ralph wandered down to the rocks. Down here, almost on a level with the sea, you could follow with your eye the the ceaseless, (3) _____ passage of the deep sea waves. They were miles wide, apparently not breakers or the banked ridges of shallow water. They travelled the length of the island with an air of disregarding it and being set on other business; they were less a progress than a (4) _____ rise and fall of the whole ocean. Now the sea would (5) _____ down, making cascades and waterfalls of retreating water, would sink past the rocks and plaster down the seaweed like (6) _____ hair: then pausing, gather and rise with a roar, irresistibly swelling over point and outcrop, climbing the little cliff, sending at last an arm of surf up a gully to end a yard or so from him in (7) _____ of spray.

Wave after wave, Ralph followed the rise and fall until something of the (8) _____ of the sea numbed his brain. Then gradually the almost infinite size of this water forced itself on his attention. This was the divider, the barrier. On the other size of the island, (9) _____ at midday with mirage, defended by the (10) _____ of the quiet lagoon, one might dream of rescue; but here, faced by the brute obtuseness of the ocean, the miles of division, one was clamped down, one was helpless, one was condemned, one was …

© Cambridge University Press 2010     Unit 7 ○ **Dislocation**    39

# Worksheet for Text 7B: The causeway

Choose the best word from the three choices to fill each blank.

On the causeway path it was still quite dry underfoot but to my left I saw that the water had begun to (1) _____ nearer, quite silent now, quite slow. I wondered how deeply the path went under water when the tide was at its (2) _____ . But on a still night such as this, there was plenty of time to cross in safety, though the distance was greater, now I was (3) _____ it on foot, than it had seemed when we trotted over in Keckwick's pony cart, and the end of the causeway path seemed to be receding into the (4) _____ ahead. I had never been quite so alone, nor felt quite so small and (5) _____ in a vast landscape before, and I fell into a brooding, philosophical frame of mind, struck by the absolute indifference of water and sky to my presence.

Some minutes later, I could not tell how many, I came out of my reverie, to realize that I could no longer see very far in front of me, and when I turned around I was (6) _____ to find that Eel Marsh House, too, was invisible, not because the darkness of evening had fallen, but because of a thick, damp sea-mist that had come (7) _____ over the marshes and (8) _____ everything, myself, the house behind me, the end of the causeway path and the countryside ahead. It was a mist like a damp, (9) _____ cobwebby thing, fine and yet impenetrable … I felt confused, teased by it, as though it were made up of millions of live fingers that crept over me, hung onto me and then (10) _____ away again. Above all, it was the suddenness of it that had so unnerved and disorientated me.

| 1 | drift | seep | creep |
| --- | --- | --- | --- |
| 2 | height | maximum | highest |
| 3 | crossing | covering | traversing |
| 4 | blackness | whiteness | greyness |
| 5 | insignificant | unimportant | lost |
| 6 | surprised | puzzled | startled |
| 7 | flooding | rolling | flowing |
| 8 | enveloped | shrouded | hid |
| 9 | sticky | transparent | clinging |
| 10 | shifted | moved | ran |

# Answers – Unit 7

**1** How writers create the effect of alienation:

The persona is alone; climate, vegetation or wildlife is different from what they are used to and extreme; the place is not at all what they were expecting; aspects of the place are personified; the weather or environment is threatening; the atmosphere is tense with expectation of an impending event; the arrival has been long awaited after an arduous journey; the persona is dreading what they will find there; the persona feels unwell, physically or psychically; the persona will not be able to leave the place because of its isolation or lack of transport.

**2** Islands:

Probable responses, because these are traditional in literature and films (e.g. the television series *Lost*), are isolation; lack of food; lack of comforts; lack of means of escape; lack of communication; fear of natives/other groups; dangerous animals; poisonous vegetation; division and fighting among the group; medical emergency; disappearances; supernatural events.

**7** The Amazon:

Tropical rivers and jungle conjure up images of watchers among the foliage; piranhas, crocodiles and other predators in the water; alarming screeching noises of parrots and exotic animals; humid and dark atmosphere; lurid green vegetation; powerful creepers and tall/thick trees full of dangerous creatures, including snakes; the idea of the unknown and unknowable in the heart of the jungle.

**12** Text 7C: effects of underlined words:

sun being very low – light is going/darkness is coming; this is a bad time to arrive in a strange place

suspicious ripples – suggestions of something dangerous moving under the water; not naming it makes it more frightening

caution was the word – this implies that there are a lot of things one must be careful of

high sides like a railway cutting – it would be impossible to escape by climbing

changed into stone and like a trance – remind the reader of bewitchment and spells

it seemed unnatural – this implies that the stillness is supernatural and that something will happen because of it, and because of the silence

struck you blind – this is a violent image, showing the power of darkness to remove the ability to see

as though a gun had been fired – this simile introduces the idea of danger and death

a white fog – another image of blindness, which always makes someone feel vulnerable to attack by something unseen

towering multitude of trees ... the immense matted jungle – these make the vegetation seem gigantic and easily able to defeat or swallow humans

greased grooves – this alliterative phrase shows how swiftly the fog returned, like the action of a gun

as of infinite desolation – the cry sounds inhuman and unbearably tragic; it creates an impression of belonging to something unearthly and desperate

# Stylistic effects

## Unit 8 Revisiting

**Topic outline**

- **Syllabus component:** Paper 2 question 2; Paper 3 section 2 question 3
- **Main skills:** identifying writers' effects; forming an overview
- **Secondary skills:** descriptive structure; descriptive language
- **Outcome:** analysis of writers' effects; *descriptive composition
- **Materials:** novel opening; descriptive writing structure handout
- **Texts:** Text 8: Dream visit

## Lesson plan

1  What kind of things would students comment on if they visited in a dream somewhere they used to know well but hadn't seen for many years? Elicit the idea of contrast between then and now, and between dream and reality. (5)

2  Ask students to read Text 8. Ask for one adjective from each to describe the overall atmosphere of the place (e.g. *forbidding, menacing, overwhelming, seductive*). Judge the best, giving reasons. (5)

3  Ask students, in pairs, to identify and underline the words and phrases in Text 8 which create atmosphere. Check choices are appropriate. (10)

4  Ask students to re-read Text 8. Ask for one adjective from each to describe the overall feeling of the persona (e.g. *nostalgic, melancholic, rejected*). Judge the best, giving reasons. (5)

5  Ask students, in pairs, to identify and highlight/ underline (in a different colour) the words and phrases in Text 8 which create feeling. Check choices are appropriate. (10)

6  Put the following adjectives from Text 8 on the board and ask students to suggest a range of synonyms for them (using a thesaurus if necessary): *forlorn, stealthy, squat, masked, malevolent*. (10)

7  Put the suggested synonyms on the board next to the original words. Is the meaning exactly the same? Discuss whether they have the same connotations or not, and why the writer chose the original words. (10)

8  Ask students to look at the opening of Text 8 and to identify the structure of the description (i.e. moving from gate, to drive, to outside of house). Explain how this movement towards the object/ place to be described is a framework which can give shape to descriptive compositions (see CD-ROM for descriptive writing structure handout). (5)

9  Ask students to use this technique to write their own opening to a descriptive composition about a building they are revisiting after several years. They should write about half a page or two paragraphs. Go around class offering support with ideas. (15)

10  Invite students to read out their openings, and ask class to comment on how well they lead the reader into the composition. (10)

11  Ask students to brainstorm a list of vocabulary to use in their descriptive composition. Encourage the selection of unusual, powerful, precise, exotic-sounding, emotive words and figurative language (e.g. similes, personification). (5)

## Homework task

Using your notes for tasks 2 to 7, write between a side and a side and a half in response to the question: How does the writer of Text 8 a) make effective the description of the garden, and b) convey the feelings of the persona?

## Additional task

Ask students to use their opening from task 9 and vocabulary list from task 11 to write a descriptive composition beginning *Last night I dreamt I went to ....* Tell them not to end with *And then I woke up* but with a more original final sentence, which could refer to movement away from the place or a statement of feeling about the experience.

# Text 8

# Dream visit

Last night I dreamt I went to Manderley again. It seemed to me I stood by the iron gate leading to the drive, and for a while I could not enter, for the way was barred to me. There was a padlock and a chain upon the gate. I called in my dream to the lodge-keeper, and had no answer, and peering closer through the rusted spokes of the gate I saw that the lodge was uninhabited.

No smoke came from the chimney, and the little lattice windows gaped forlorn. Then, like all dreamers, I was possessed of a sudden with supernatural powers and passed like a spirit through the barrier before me. The drive wound away in front of me, twisting and turning as it had always done, but as I advanced I was aware that a change had come upon it; it was narrow and unkempt, not the drive that we had known. At first I was puzzled and did not understand, and it was only when I bent my head to avoid the low swinging branch of a tree that I realised what had happened. Nature had come into her own again and, little by little, in her stealthy, insidious way had encroached upon the drive with long, tenacious fingers. The woods, always a menace even in the past, had triumphed in the end. They crowded, dark and uncontrolled, to the borders of the drive. The beeches with white, naked limbs leant close to one another, their branches intermingled in a strange embrace, making a vault above my head like the archway of a church. And there were other trees as well, trees that I did not recognise, squat oaks and tortured elms that straggled cheek by jowl with the beeches, and had thrust themselves out of the quiet earth, along with monster shrubs and plants, none of which I remembered.

The drive was a ribbon now, a thread of its former self, with gravel surface gone, and choked with grass and moss. The trees had thrown out low branches, making an impediment to progress; the gnarled roots looked like skeleton claws. Scattered here and there amongst this jungle growth I would recognise shrubs that had been landmarks in our time, things of culture and grace, hydrangeas whose blue heads had been famous. No hand had checked their progress, and they had gone native now, rearing to a monster height without a bloom, black and ugly as the nameless parasites that grew beside them.

On and on, now east now west, wound the poor thread than once had been our drive. Sometimes I thought it lost, but it appeared again, beneath a fallen tree perhaps, or struggling on the other side of a muddied ditch created by the winter rains. I had not thought the way so long. Surely the miles had multiplied, even as the trees had done, and this path led but to a labyrinth, some choked wilderness, and not a house at all. I came upon it suddenly; the approach was masked by the unnatural growth of a vast shrub that spread in all directions, and I stood, my heart thumping in my breast, the strange prick of tears behind my eyes. [...]

The garden had obeyed the jungle law, even as the woods had done. [...] A lilac had mated with a copper beech, and to bind them yet more closely to one another the malevolent ivy, always an enemy to grace, had thrown her tendrils about the pair and made them prisoners. [...] Nettles were everywhere, the vanguard of the army. They choked the terrace, they sprawled about the paths, they leant, vulgar and lanky, against the very windows of the house. [...]

A cloud, hitherto unseen, came upon the moon, and hovered an instant like a dark hand before a face. [...] The house was a sepulchre, our fear and suffering lay buried in the ruins. There would be no resurrection.

Source: *Rebecca* by Daphne Du Maurier, Virago, 2003.

# Answers – Unit 8

**3**  Text 8: words and phrases creating atmosphere:

*rusted; uninhabited; narrow and unkempt; stealthy, insidious; long, tenacious fingers; menace; triumphed; crowded, dark and uncontrolled; squat; tortured; monster; choked; gnarled; like skeleton claws; black and ugly; nameless parasites; labyrinth; choked wilderness; masked; jungle law; malevolent ivy; enemy to grace; prisoners; army; vulgar and lanky; a dark hand before a face; a sepulchre; buried in the ruins; no resurrection*

The use of the device of anthropomorphism (giving the vegetation human qualities), battle imagery, vocabulary associated with death and suffocation, the idea of denied entrance and hindered progress, the repetition of certain powerful words (e.g. *choked*) all contribute to the atmosphere of a place growing out of control and threatening to humans. The choice of dark flowerless plants which are parasites or weeds – *ivy, nettles* – is also symptomatic of the sinisterness of the place.

**5**  Text 8: words and phrases conveying feeling:

*barred; forlorn; I was puzzled; trees that I did not recognise; none of which I remembered; I had not thought the way so long; my heart thumping in my breast; prick of tears behind my eyes; fear and suffering; no resurrection*

These words add up to an overall feeling by the persona that she is lonely, excluded and unwelcome in this place; that the past is not accessible to her. Some of the words describing human feeling have been attributed to parts of the building (e.g. *forlorn*), and this transference of adjectives connects the persona and the place, making it more animate (alive) and her more inanimate (dead). The fusion of the atmosphere of a graveyard and the feeling of hopelessness in the phrase *no resurrection* intensifies the relationship between the woman and the house, and the emotional power of the passage.

**6**  Text 8: synonyms (in rank order of low to high intensity):

***forlorn*** *– lonely, abandoned, forsaken, desolate, bereft*

***stealthy*** *– slow, undetectable, surreptitious, secretive, furtive*

***squat*** *– short, thick, low, square, compact*

***masked*** *– covered, hidden, unidentifiable, concealed, disguised*

***malevolent*** *– hateful, ill-wishing, spiteful, vicious, evil*

# Summary

## Unit 9 Missing persons

### Topic outline

- **Syllabus component:** Paper 1; Paper 2 question 3
- **Main skills:** selecting material, sequencing material, summary style
- **Secondary skills:** vocabulary building; concision; paraphrasing; making inferences; news reporting; *narrative writing
- **Outcome:** summaries; news report; *narrative composition
- **Materials:** informative texts; summary writing process handout
- **Texts:** Text 9A: Jim Thompson's house; Text 9B: Silken dreams; Text 9C: The piano man

### Lesson plan

1. Ask students to read Text 9A. (5)

2. Ask for synonyms for the 15 words in bold in the text. Comment on responses. (10)

3. Ask students to re-read the text and highlight information about Jim Thompson's house. Ask them to make a list of the points, in their own words as far as possible, and to group/order them. (10)

4. Read out points to be included while students check and correct their lists. Ask students to write a one-paragraph summary of Jim Thompson's house, using complex sentences and avoiding the use of *and* as far as possible. (See CD-ROM for summary writing process handout.) (10)

5. Invite students to read their paragraphs to the class, to be judged for concision of style. (5)

6. Read Text 9B while students follow text and underline unknown words. (5)

7. Ask students to guess the meanings of unknown words using the recommended methods (i.e. breaking down words into constituent parts, family word connections, other language similarities, logical guess from context). (5)

8. Ask students to re-read Texts 9A and 9B and to select and list the biographical facts about Jim Thompson. (5)

9. Ask students, in pairs, to compare selections and agree on a list of relevant facts. (5)

10. Ask the students to sequence the points in their list and use it to write a half-page summary of Jim Thompson's life. They should write in complex sentences, avoiding the use of *and*. (15)

11. Ask students to check the accuracy of their summaries. Collect them to assess for content (15 points) and style (5 points for concision, focus and own words). (5)

12. Ask students to read out Text 9C, one point each. (5)

13. Invite students to offer theories about the identity of the piano man, making inferences from the information in Text 9C. The class can judge which is the most convincing. (5)

### Homework task

Expand and reorder the summary notes in Text 9C into continuous informative prose.

### Additional task

Ask students to imagine they are a Hollywood screenwriter and to write the story of what happened to Jim Thompson, using the facts about his disappearance as the basis for a film script, entitled 'Missing Person'.

# Text 9A

# Jim Thompson's house

You are now in the Thai home of Jim Thompson, an American who was born in Greenville, Delaware, in 1906. A practising architect prior to World War II, he volunteered for service in the US Army, **campaigned** in Europe, and came to Asia as part of the force that hoped to help restore Thailand's full freedom and independence. However, the war ended before he saw action. He arrived in Bangkok a short time later as a military intelligence officer attached to the O.S.S.* After leaving the service, he decided to return and live in Thailand permanently.

The hand weaving of silk, a long-neglected cottage industry, captured Jim Thompson's attention, and he devoted himself to **reviving** the craft. Highly gifted as a designer and textile colourist, he contributed **substantially** to the industry's growth and to the worldwide recognition **accorded** to Thai silk.

He gained further **renown** through the construction of this house, combining six teak buildings which represented the best in traditional Thai architecture. Most of the houses were at least two centuries old; they were easily **dismantled** and brought to the present site, some from as far away as the old capital of Ayudhya.

In his **quest** for **authenticity**, Jim Thompson **adhered** to the customs of the early builders in most respects. The houses were **elevated** a full storey above the ground, a practical Thai **precaution** to avoid flooding during the rainy season, and the roof tiles were fired in Ayudhya employing a design common centuries ago but rarely used today. The red paint on the outside walls is a preservative often found on old Thai buildings. The chandeliers were a **concession** to modern convenience, but even they belong to a past era, having come from 18th- and 19th-century Bangkok palaces.

All the traditional religious rituals were followed during construction of the house, and on a spring day in 1959, decreed as being **auspicious** by astrologers, Jim Thompson moved in. The house and the art collection soon became such a point of interest that he decided to open his home to the public, with **proceeds** donated to Thai charities and to projects directed towards the preservation of Thailand's rich cultural heritage.

On 26th March 1967, Jim Thompson disappeared while on a visit to the Cameron Highlands in Malaysia. Not a single valid clue has turned up in the **ensuing** years as to what might have happened to him. His famous Thai house, however, remains as a lasting reminder of his creative ability and his deep love of Thailand.

Source: James H.W. Thompson Foundation

*O.S.S. – organisation which became the C.I.A.

# Text 9B

# Silken dreams

James Thompson arrived in Thailand as an American military intelligence officer at the end of the Second World War. He decided to stay in the country but was divorced by his wife who did not wish to live in Southeast Asia. The former architect from Delaware began by renovating the celebrated Oriental Hotel in Bangkok, which had been damaged during the Japanese occupation. While he was doing this, Thompson had become fascinated by Thailand's rich, exotic, hand-woven silks and he set about reviving the declining cottage industry. His skill as a designer and textile colourist was noted by fashion editors and film producers, which led to the creation of his empire founded on silk.

But Thompson was not to enjoy his dream for long. On 26th March 1967, while he was visiting some friends in the Cameron Highlands, Malaysia, they went for a picnic on Mount Brinchang. His friends returned home, but Thompson vanished. The area contains wild, untamed jungle, but Thompson was familiar with such terrain from his survival training when a commando. It drops steeply down into a valley shrouded in oaks, laurels, cinnamon trees and rhododendrons. There is an overgrown trail which leads to the Lutheran Mission where Thompson was last seen. The person who last saw Thompson remembers that he had a camera around his neck. He turned to wave goodbye and was never seen again.

Search parties, including police, soldiers and helicopters, were mobilised, scouring a 100-kilometre area of jungle and mountains. A 25,000-dollar reward was offered. Even tribal witchdoctors and mind-readers were consulted, but after ten days the operation was called off. Locals suggested a tiger attack; a tiger had been recently witnessed making off with a dog from the same spot. But tiger attacks usually leave something behind, perhaps a belt buckle or shoes. Others believe he was accidentally shot by a tribal blow-dart. But less than six months later, his elderly sister was murdered in America, which added to the mystery. Two or three people go missing each year in this area of misty highlands, but they are generally found within a few days once the tribal trackers are sent out. No one else has ever vanished without trace in the area, which gives a chilling poignancy to Thompson's case.

During the following months the case was characterised by false alarms, mystical visions and bizarre theories. Even aliens were blamed for his disappearance. Some investigators favoured the idea of a communist kidnapping plot, as there were terrorists active throughout the 450 square kilometres of the Cameron Highlands until they finally surrendered in 1989. Thompson disappeared at the height of the Vietnam War, when the USA was battling communism, and there were rumours that he was still working for the American CIA. It also emerged after his death that he had fallen out with the Thailand Society and had removed them from his will. There were reported sightings of Thompson in places as far apart as Canton, Laos and Tahiti, but finally in 1974 Thompson was declared dead in the USA and Thailand. His file, however, is still open in the nearby police station, labelled 'Missing in action'. His famous house in Bangkok now resembles the *Marie Celeste*, untouched exactly as he left it. Forty years have offered no further clues to this mystery, which is worthy of treatment by Hollywood's most imaginative scriptwriters.

# Text 9C

# The piano man

- found by police on east coast of England in April
- wandering on a beach in the dark
- he refuses to speak
- he is blond and in his twenties
- so nicknamed because he drew grand pianos when given paper by hospital staff
- was wearing a soaking wet dinner jacket when found
- he is physically fit and uninjured
- his psychiatric treatment in a hospital in Kent is very expensive
- he plays classical music for hours on the piano in the hospital chapel
- he writes music and carries it around with him
- he refuses to wear any other clothes
- he cries sometimes
- he cowers and becomes extremely agitated if approached
- he becomes relaxed only when playing the piano
- he refuses to watch television or listen to the radio
- labels on his clothing had been removed
- his case has made headlines round the world
- he has baffled police, health care workers and psychiatrists
- he escaped once but was found by police and returned to the hospital
- nearly a thousand people have rung the Missing Persons helpline claiming they recognised his newspaper photograph, but they were all wrong

# Answers – Unit 9

**3** Relevant information about Jim Thompson's house:
- consists of six teak buildings
- traditional Thai architecture
- most parts of house at least two centuries old
- taken apart and moved to present site
- some parts came from the old capital of Ayudhya
- raised on stilts to prevent flooding
- roof tiles made according to an ancient method
- coloured with preservative red paint
- chandeliers came from old palaces in Bangkok
- religious rituals were observed during construction

**4** One-paragraph summary of Jim Thompson's house:

Jim Thompson's house in Bankgok consists of six teak buildings in traditional Thai architectural style, most of them at least two centuries old. The buildings were taken apart and moved to the present site, some from the former capital of Ayudhya and the chandeliers from old palaces in Bangkok. The building is elevated on stilts to prevent flooding, and preserved by red paint. The roof tiles were made according to the ancient method; tradition was also followed by the observance of religious rituals during the construction of the house.

**8** Biographical facts about Jim Thompson:
- full name James H.W. Thompson
- an American born in Delaware in 1906
- formerly an architect
- a military intelligence officer
- arrived in Thailand at the end of Second World War
- became divorced from his American wife
- restored the Oriental Hotel in Bangkok
- a traditionalist
- inspired by Thai silk and facilitated the growth of the industry
- a gifted textile designer
- the fashion and film industry used his products
- generous to Thai cultural charities
- visited Malaysia in March 1967
- disappeared on 26th March on a solitary afternoon walk
- had trained as a commando in jungle territory
- was interested in photography
- had an elder sister living in America, who was murdered
- was declared dead in 1974
- the only person to have ever been permanently lost in this area
- no clues or evidence exist to explain his disappearance

**10** Half-page summary of Jim Thompson's life:

James H.W. Thompson, born in Delaware USA in 1906, was an architect before he became a military intelligence officer in the Second World War. After he arrived in Thailand at the end of the war his wife left him and he settled in Bangkok, where he did restoration work on its most famous hotel, The Oriental. He reconstructed a house for himself using traditional materials and methods, devoting the proceeds from allowing visitors to the house to Thai cultural charities. His gift for textile design brought him to the attention of the fashion and film industries, thereby making his name and revitalising the Thai silk industry.

On a visit to friends in Malaysia, in the spring of 1967, he vanished in the jungle – although this was terrain he was familiar with from his military training – carrying a camera. Shortly after his disappearance his elder sister was murdered in America. Thompson was declared dead in 1974, and remains the only person to have ever been permanently lost in the Cameron Highlands, provoking a vast array of theories to explain his disappearance, none of which have been proven.

# Summary

## Unit 10 Pretend friends

### Topic outline

- **Syllabus component:** Paper 2 question 3; Paper 3 section 1
- **Main skills:** summary; style analysis
- **Secondary skills:** vocabulary building; advertising language; complex sentences
- **Outcome:** advertisement; summary; *interview script
- **Materials:** newspaper and Internet news reports; Worksheet for Text 10A: Maid in Japan
- **Texts:** Text 10A: Maid in Japan; Text 10B: Give us a smile!

### Lesson plan

1. Ask students how they feel about robots. Should they be made to look and behave as humanly as possible? What should they be used for? What are the advantages and disadvantages of their having been invented? (5)

2. Ask students to read Text 10A and to each say in one sentence what it is about. (5)

3. Give out Worksheet for Text 10A and ask students to complete it. (15)

4. Ask students to swap worksheets to mark. Give answers. (10)

5. Ask students to find examples of advertising style and vocabulary in Text 10A, and to explain what effect they have in this context. (5)

6. Elicit features of advertising style (i.e. multiple adjectives, imperatives, rhetorical questions, aspirational vocabulary, positive associations, future tense) and write on board. Ask students to write a one-paragraph TV or magazine advertisement for Wakamaru. (10)

7. Invite students to read out their paragraphs. Comment on how informative and persuasive they are. (10)

8. Ask students to read Text 10B and make notes, in two columns, on its similarities to and differences from Text 10A in content and style. (10)

9. Invite answers and discuss them. (5)

10. Ask students to write one complex sentence, in their own words, describing how the humanoid robotic head is able to copy human facial expressions. (5)

11. Invite students to read out their sentences. Comment on accuracy, concision and use of own words. (5)

12. Ask students to collect points from Texts 10A and 10B for the following summary questions: a) What are the possible benefits of owning Wakamaru or Jules? b) What are the possible drawbacks? (5)

### Homework task

Turn your list from task 12 into a one-page summary – after making sure that you have at least 15 points – and check it for clarity and concision of expression.

### Additional task

Ask students to write a script for a radio programme on the topic of the latest technological inventions, in which an interviewer asks Ken Onishi, creator of Wakamaru, and Neill Campbell, chief researcher for Jules, how they can justify the creation of humanoid robots despite their dangers and drawbacks. They should include all the relevant information from both Text 10A and Text 10B in the interview, which should begin: *Interviewer: So tell me, Mr Onishi, how this new product from Japan is different from previous household robots ...*

# Text 10A

# Maid in Japan

WANTED: RELIABLE, UNPAID PERSONAL ORGANISER WITHOUT EMOTIONAL COMPLICATIONS. No problem; just wheel in Wakamaru. She may not look entirely as you would expect, with a shiny face of canary yellow and metallic arms a delicate shade of silver, but this smooth-talking Japanese lady has the potential to be the ideal companion.

For those with a tendency to feel sluggish of a morning, she can glide to your bedside armed with the news headlines and the weather forecast. For the organisationally challenged, she will willingly fill you in on the contents of your diary. And if you're looking a little **rotund**, she will urge you to fit in a light jogging session before you start the day.

Friendly, charming and absolutely dependable, Wakamaru is all you ever wanted in an assistant. Within days she could become an immovable fixture in your life. The only thing is, she's a robot. Wakamaru, the latest futuristic product to be **unveiled** by Mitsubishi, is the walking, talking result of a Japanese programme aiming to create a robot that comes as close as possible to a real person. The metre-high humanoid is capable of recognising up to 10 individuals by name and greeting friends and family in a soothing, gentle voice that betrays only the slightest hint of being chip-induced.

'We have tried to create a robot you can have a relationship with, just like a human,' Ken Onishi, the technical team leader in charge of designing Wakamaru, said yesterday. While none of her features are entirely **revolutionary**, the robot's overall package was a colossal task for designers, Mr Onishi explained. Even in Japan, a country at the forefront of innovation in the robotic field, putting together a machine capable of combining all Wakamaru's skills is an incredible feat of science.

The team at Mitsubishi claims the Internet-linked robot, as well as being able to take phone messages and read out any emails that may have dropped into her owner's inbox, has a programmed personality designed to **ape** as far as possible the warmth and friendliness of a real human being. It has even been suggested that she is sufficiently adaptable to make her a suitable carer for elderly people with nobody else to look after them. Her frame contains an internal alarm system programmed to call emergency services if a person has an accident. Speech-recognition software and a built-in dictionary provide Wakamaru's vocabulary.

The only **snag** is that, like most good things in life, Wakamaru does not come cheap. A limited edition of 100 robots goes on sale today in Tokyo for about a million euros. As demanding as any other lady of style, she also requires a high monthly maintenance charge.

Source: Elizabeth Davies, *The Independent*, 16th September 2005.

# Text 10B

## Give us a smile!

Scientists have created the first 'humanoid' robot that can mimic the facial expressions and lip movements of a human being. 'Jules' – a disembodied androgynous robotic head – can automatically copy the movements picked up by a video camera and mapped on to the tiny electronic motors in its skin. It can grin and grimace, furrow its brow and speak as the software translates the expressions observed on a video camera into digital commands that make the robot produce mirrored movements. It all happens in real time, as the robot can interpret the commands at 25 frames per second.

The animatronic head has flexible rubber skin that is moved by 34 servo motors, which trigger commands to produce similarly realistic facial movements. The technology works using ten stock human emotions. Copycat robot heads have been created before, but not with realistic human-looking faces. Jules' human appearance makes getting the expressions perfect even more critical, to avoid the notorious 'uncanny valley', a term to describe the way that human-like robots that are not quite true-to-life are perceived as more unnerving and alarming than less realistic more mechanical-looking versions. 'We are really attuned to how a face moves, and if it's slightly wrong it gives us a feeling that the head is somehow creepy,' explains Neill Campbell, the scientist who devised and led the research at the Bristol Robotics Laboratory in the west of England. It took a team of three engineers three and a half years to develop the breakthrough software to create interaction between humans and artificial intelligence.

Reaching the other side of the 'uncanny valley' – achieving such realism that people react to robots as they do to humans – would have significant benefits, says Campbell. Human communication relies heavily on facial expressions, so robots that can mimic them well should find much wider application. He anticipates that this would make them useful in healthcare settings, such as nursing homes, and predicts that one day robotic companions will work or assist humans in space – or any other field where trustworthiness, reliability and emotional intelligence are required.

However, not everyone is impressed by Jules' master of mimicry, and some scientists question the ethical implications of using human-like robots for more than entertainment. They fear that exposed or vulnerable people, like children or the elderly, would be disconcerted by humanoid automatons. They might be fooled into trying to form a social relationship with the robot – thinking that it is capable of not only looking like a human and behaving like a human, but also feeling like a human – or react negatively towards a robot which just looks too human.

# Worksheet for Text 10A: Maid in Japan

**1** Give the meaning of the underlined phrases in the passage. [5]

tendency to feel sluggish: _____

organisationally challenged: _____

chip-induced: _____

overall package: _____

the forefront of innovation: _____

**2** Give synonyms for the bolded words in the passage. [5]

rotund: _____

unveiled: _____

revolutionary: _____

ape: _____

snag: _____

**3** Find words in the passage which mean: [5]

possibility: _____

move smoothly: _____

encourage: _____

totally: _____

permanent: _____

calming: _____

suggestion: _____

huge: _____

achievement: _____

versatile: _____

# Answers to Worksheet for Text 10A

**1** Give the meaning of the underlined phrases in the passage. [5]

tendency to feel sluggish: **liking for staying in bed, dislike of getting up**

organisationally challenged: **poor managers, inefficient planners**

chip-induced: **computer-generated**

overall package: **complete range of elements**

the forefront of innovation: **the leaders/in the vanguard of invention**

**2** Give synonyms for the bolded words in the passage. [5]

rotund: **round, overweight**

unveiled: **revealed, released**

revolutionary: **radical, novel**

ape: **mimic, copy**

snag: **difficulty, drawback**

**3** Find words in the passage which mean: [5]

possibility: **potential**

move smoothly: **glide**

encourage: **urge**

totally: **absolutely**

permanent: **immovable**

calming: **soothing**

suggestion: **hint**

huge: **colossal**

achievement: **feat**

versatile: **adaptable**

# Answers – Unit 10

**2** Text 10A: one-sentence summary:

In Japan, a new type of robot has been launched, which can perform a wider range of human-support tasks than has been possible before.

**3** See Worksheet for Text 10A answers.

**5** Text 10A: advertising style:

The following phrases are typical of advertising: *No problem* (minimising difficulties); *a delicate shade of silver* (focus on attractive colour); *the ideal companion* (suggesting perfection); *a little rotund* (euphemism to avoid giving offence); *Friendly, charming and absolutely dependable* (triple adjectival structure, plus an absolute adverb); *Wakamaru is all you ever wanted* (extreme claim); *walking, talking* (typical rhyming phrase); *only the slightest hint* (playing down a negative); *an incredible feat of science* (exaggeration to impress); *does not come cheap* (understatement to avoid mentioning the off-putting word *expensive*). Text 10A begins with a Wanted ad and then uses an imperative, a non-sentence, and a sentence beginning with *And*. These are all syntactical features of adverts.

**6** One-paragraph advert for Wakamaru:

Be the envy of your friends with this latest household appliance. She's more than a gadget; she's more than a maid; she's more than a personal assistant: she's a friend. Life will be brighter and easier if you share your home with dependable, efficient, cheerful Wakamaru, the ultimate in advanced technology.

**8** Comparison of Texts 10A and 10B:

**Similarities**: both are concerned with a newly developed robot which has human characteristics and which could be used to assist humans in the types of workplace where empathy and reliability are required.

**Differences**: these take the form of the gender and appearance of the robots, the countries where they were developed, and the fears about the possible reaction to them. The styles of the texts are also different, the first being quite lighthearted and colloquial, the second being serious and scientific in register.

**10** One sentence describing how Jules works:

The head is able to mimic in real time, with its flexible rubber skin, the human expressions captured on a video camera and mapped on to the tiny electronic motors in its skin by software which translates the expressions into digital commands to the robot's 34 servo-motors.

**12** Summary points: [26 points]

**a**
Benefits of Wakamaru:
- ideal companion
- brings you news and weather
- runs your diary
- advises exercise
- charming
- reliable
- recognises your family and friends
- greets your visitors
- takes phone messages and relays emails
- friendly personality
- able to be a carer
- can call for help in emergency

Benefits of Jules:
- realistic face and expressions
- speed of response to human expressions
- range of emotions portrayed
- use in healthcare or education
- use in areas requiring reliability, like space travel
- can have empathic relationship with humans

**b**
Drawbacks of Wakamaru:
- strange appearance
- expensive to buy
- expensive to maintain

Drawbacks of Jules:
- it's only a head
- it is neither male nor female
- expressions can look alarming if not quite right
- humans can be tricked into thinking Jules has feeling
- may look too human and provoke a negative reaction

# Summary

## Unit 11 Sharks and crocs!

**Topic outline**

- **Syllabus component:** Paper 2 question 3; Paper 3 section 1; Paper 6 individual task
- **Main skills:** summary
- **Secondary skills:** selecting material; paragraphing; news report style; summary style
- **Outcome:** news bulletin; summary; leaflet; *interview; *formal talk
- **Materials:** news reports from Internet, newspapers and news agency
- **Texts:** Text 11A: Trojan shark project; Texts 11B, 11C, 11D: Crocodile reports; Text 11E: Shark myths and facts

## Lesson plan

1. Ask students to skim-read Text 11A and say, in one sentence, what the passage is about. (5)

2. Ask students, in pairs, to scan Text 11A for summary points about a) the Trojan shark and b) real sharks, highlighting them in different colours. Write points on board in two columns. (10)

3. Ask students, in pairs, to link with brackets several short paragraphs into one longer paragraph in Text 11A. (5)

4. Invite students to explain their decisions, giving reasons. Ask them why news reports use unusually short paragraphs. (5)

5. Ask students to skim-read Texts 11B, 11C and 11D and comment on the three headlines. (10)

6. Ask students, in pairs, to scan Texts 11B, 11C and 11D for facts about a) present-day and b) pre-historic crocodiles, highlighting them in different colours in two columns. Write points on board. (10)

7. Ask students to remove unnecessary words and form one complex sentence from the first four sentences of Text 11B. (5)

8. Invite responses, and suggestions why news reports use shorter and simpler sentences than summaries. (5)

9. Ask students to reduce and reorder Text 11C to turn it into a radio news bulletin of one paragraph. (10)

10. Choose students to read out their bulletins. Comment as a class on the suitability of content (only key facts), style (concise) and register (formal). (5)

11. Ask students to read Text 11E, to order and combine the points, and to write a half-page summary, in complex sentences, of the facts and myths about sharks. (15)

12. Ask students to edit and improve their summaries by removing repetition, clarifying points, using more of their own words, and linking sentences. Collect the summaries for assessment (see Paper 2 mark scheme on the CIE Teacher Support website). (5)

### Homework task

Using material from Texts 11A and 11E, plan and write a leaflet for the Shark Protection Society, which should be one side of writing. The task is informative, and this should be reflected in the style.

### Additional tasks

a. Ask students to write and perform a dialogue between one of Jeremy Doble's parents and a local radio presenter. They should begin the dialogue: *People are amazed that you decided you did not want the crocodile which killed your son to be killed. Can you explain to listeners why you took that decision?* Dialogues will be judged according to their level of informativeness and the appropriateness of their style/register.

b. Ask students to write a talk in the role of a manager of a crocodile park to explain how to avoid being attacked by crocodiles.

# Text 11A

# The Trojan shark project

Deep beneath the waves a weird fish has swallowed the grandson of the late Captain Jacques Cousteau, the ocean explorer. Fabien Cousteau, 36, is these days to be found inside the belly of a submersible built in the shape of a Great White shark.

It might seem a foolhardy enterprise, but Cousteau is using the robotic fish to get as close as possible to real Great Whites, the most ferocious killers of the sea, in the hope of filming them without disturbing their natural behaviour.

The 'Trojan shark', built from steel and plastic, is 4 metres long and was created by a Hollywood prop expert at a cost of £115,000.

'The whole point,' says Cousteau, 'is to fool them into thinking I am a shark.'

It is hardly the most comforting of environments in which to get cosy with the predatory fish. Cousteau's diving contraption is covered with Skinflex, a malleable material mixed with glass beads and sand to simulate the texture of shark skin, right down to the ugly scars that commonly disfigure the biggest Great Whites.

The head swings open on hinges to allow Cousteau to enter the body. There he lies flat, holding a joystick in each hand to control speed, left and right movement, and pitch – 'just like a fighter plane,' he says.

The shark's eyes are camera lenses and a third camera is positioned in a rubber 'pilot fish' clamped, in another lifelike touch, to the underbelly of the submarine.

A 'pneumatic propulsion system' invented by the American navy powers the shark's tail. It enables it to move quietly and without creating bubbles.

'Bubbles make noise the sharks would feel and hear,' explains Cousteau. 'It's an artificial stimulus that could spook them or alter their behaviour in some way.'

Unsettling Great Whites is inadvisable. They have been blamed for three deaths this year and numerous attacks on swimmers and surfers. Some have been known to attack the metal cages used by divers. In the image popularised by the Steven Spielberg film *Jaws*, a Great White is even thought capable of biting a small boat in half.

With the Trojan shark, Cousteau is protected by a stainless steel skeleton made from 5 cm thick ribs beneath the shark's skin.

Perhaps because of their fearsome reputation, the Great White remains little understood. Scientists have yet to establish where they breed, how long they live and how big they can grow. The largest on record is 6.4 metres.

Cousteau's device has enabled him to study the fish with unprecedented insight. Over the past few months he has been filming Great Whites from Mexico to Australia for American television. His findings contradict popular conceptions.

In fact, he says, 'Great White sharks do not go around chomping up boats'. Instead he claims they are 'very timid creatures'. [...]

The new mechanical shark – called Troy but nicknamed Sushi by some of Cousteau's crew – has proved successful. Real sharks tend to accept the intruder as a dominant female, says Cousteau, even though they may be baffled by some of its features. The mouth can open and close but does not eat. And Troy, unlike real sharks, is odourless and incapable of great bursts of speed. [...]

With the help of Troy, Fabien, born in Paris but now living in New York, may become the most effective torchbearer of his grandfather's mission.

He could not have better credentials: he began diving at the age of four when his grandfather designed a junior scuba outfit for him.

He was only six when he sneaked into a cinema to watch *Jaws*, which his parents had forbidden him to see.

He says he was horrified by the film because 'it went against everything I'd ever been taught'.

That experience still underlies his desire to show audiences that sharks are not evil creatures but natural predators. He may yet change the popular perception of Great Whites, assuming Troy continues to perform as planned – and Cousteau does not end up inside the wrong shark.

Source: Matthew Campbell, *Sunday Times*, 2nd October 2005.

**Text 11B**

# Boy eaten by crocodile

The remains of a boy of five have been found inside a crocodile in Australia. Jeremy Doble had been playing with his brother Ryan, 7, and their boxer puppy near a mangrove swamp behind the family home in northern Queensland.

The boys had been towing each other on a boogie board through the waist-deep water along the bank of the rain-swollen Daintree River. The puppy entered the river, and Jeremy went in after it when he saw the huge crocodile approaching. Ryan saw Jeremy disappear under the water, and moments later saw the crocodile swimming away. Their father heard Ryan's screaming but by the time he arrived there was no sign of Jeremy.

Queensland Police today confirmed that the remains of the missing boy have been found inside a 4-metre male crocodile named Goldie, which was captured in the Daintree River during a police search near the spot where the child disappeared last week. The Queensland Environmental Protection Agency describe the river as 'prime crocodile territory', and it is believed to be home to up to 100 of the giant predators.

The killer reptile has been caught but, at the request of the boy's family, will not be killed. Jeremy's parents Steve and Sharon run a crocodile-watching tourism business, and they believe that crocodile attacks are a fact of life in northern Queensland. They explain that Goldie was one of the dominant males in the river and was simply acting on instinct – so he should not be put down. Instead, the animal will be sent to a farm or zoo, but because it has killed a human it will not be displayed.

There has been steady growth in the number of crocodiles in the region since they were protected by law in 1971. Problem reptiles which threaten humans can be killed, but first the authorities will seek the opinion of crocodile experts to ask if it would be more appropriate for them to be transported to another area.

Jeremy's death comes a mere five months after Scotsman Arthur Booker, on holiday with his wife, was killed by a 4-metre crocodile in another river in the same region.

# Crocodile George spends 6 nights up a tree

An Australian cattle rancher has told how he spent seven days up a tree looking down into the jaws of two hungry crocodiles after stumbling into a swamp crawling with the reptiles.

David George, 53, was knocked unconscious after falling from his horse during a bush-burning operation in north Queensland. Dazed and bleeding after coming round, he remounted his horse, hoping it would take him home. Instead it took him to a swamp criss-crossed by crocodile tracks.

Surrounded by 'salties' – saltwater crocodiles – Mr George realised his only chance was to climb. Injured and with just two sandwiches to sustain him, he spent the next six nights tied to a branch as the would-be man-eaters prowled below.

He was finally plucked from the boughs and winched to safety by helicopter after its pilot spotted his frantic waving and a makeshift distress signal – sunlight reflecting off his tobacco tin.

'I couldn't go back. It was too far and too dangerous. So I headed to the nearest high ground and stayed there, hoping someone would come and find me before the crocs did. Every night I was stalked by two crocs who would sit at the bottom of the tree staring up at me. All I could see was two sets of red eyes below me.'

Mr George, who manages a remote cattle station in north Queensland, told how he spent his first night in a fork in the tree around 2.5 metres from the ground, strapping himself to a branch and trying to snatch some sleep while standing up. The next night he got higher and set up some sticks that he could lie on. He lived on moisture from leaves.

Officials say he was fortunate to escape, as crocodiles are opportunistic predators who would have sensed they were within feet of injured prey and seen him as an easy next meal.

Adapted from 'My six nights up a tree' by Barbie Dutter, *Daily Telegraph*, 18th August 2007.

# Monster crocs dined on dinosaurs

A crocodile more than 10 metres long and weighing about 10 tons was the top predator in an African river 110 million years ago, and dined on large dinosaurs and other animals which came within range.

A nearly complete fossil skeleton of the monster crocodile was recently found in the desert in the African country Niger by Paul Sereno, a well-known dinosaur hunter at the University of Chicago. The creature is known as *Sarcosuchus Imperator* ('flesh crocodile emperor'), and was originally discovered by French scientists in 1964, but until now only fragments of skeletons had been found.

Sereno said that the skull of the Sarcosuchus is about 2 metres long and features long, narrow jaws containing more than 100 teeth. 'They are crushing, penetrating teeth,' he said, suggesting that the animal probably fed on land animals, whereas modern crocodiles more commonly eat fish and turtles. The animal's eye sockets would have rotated upwards, enabling it to remain submerged in water while watching the shoreline for prey.

Modern crocodiles in African rivers often seize large animals, such as wildebeest and zebras, with their powerful jaws and pull them into the water, where they are drowned before being consumed. Sarcosuchus probably did the same thing, hiding underwater with only its eyes visible until a dinosaur or other large animal came to drink; the crocodile would then lift its head and grasp the prey with its powerful jaws.

Based on an analysis of the growth rings in the animal's bony plates, Sereno estimated that the fossil was of an animal about 80% fully grown, and speculated that it would probably have taken 50 to 60 years for the animal to reach maturity.

Text 11E

# Shark myths and facts

## Myths

- sharks attack swimmers if they have come to expect to be fed by people
- all sharks are predators and they see humans as no more than shark bait
- sharks are unpredictable and attack without warning
- divers are only safe if wearing chain-mail or in cages

## Facts

- divers are merely regarded as other predators by sharks
- of the hundreds of shark species, few pose a threat
- those that are threatening are rarely seen and account for few deaths
- attacks are usually the result of mistaken identity, as a surfer looks like an injured seal
- if sharks are moving slowly and gracefully, they are not likely to attack
- cages only need to be used when a shark has been deliberately enticed to feed by 'chumming' (pouring fish blood into the water)

# Answers – Unit 11

**1** Text 11A is about the use of a manned mechanical shark which enables researchers to get closer to real sharks in order to film them, allowing them to discover new information which overturns some of the myths associated with Great White sharks.

**2** Text 11A: summary points:

  **a** Trojan shark [18 points]
- submersible in the shape of a Great White
- built from steel and plastic
- 4 metres long
- created by a Hollywood prop expert
- cost of £115,000
- skin made of malleable material which simulates texture of shark skin
- hinged head allows entrance to body
- joysticks control speed and angle
- shark's eyes are camera lenses and a third camera is positioned beneath
- American navy invention propels shark's tail
- moves quietly and without creating bubbles
- has 5 cm thick stainless steel skeleton
- named Troy but nicknamed Sushi
- mouth opens and closes but Trojan does not eat
- it is odourless
- it is unable to move fast
- device has enabled unprecedented opportunity to study sharks
- accepted by real sharks as a dominant female

  **b** real sharks [15 points]
- the most ferocious marine predators
- large ones disfigured by ugly scars
- attended by pilot fish
- blamed for several deaths and attacks on swimmers and surfers every year
- have been known to attack metal cages containing divers
- considered capable of biting a small boat in half (because of film *Jaws*)
- the Great White remains little understood
- scientists don't know where they breed, how long they live and how big they can grow
- the largest on record is 6.4 metres
- Great Whites can be found from Mexico to Australia
- many false perceptions about sharks
- sharks actually very timid
- Great White sharks do not attack and eat boats
- they have a smell
- they are capable of great speed

**4** Text 11A: paragraph joining: (there is an alternative for paragraph 15)

  1 + 2 + 4 + 15

  3 + 5 + 6 + 7

  8 + 9 + 10 + 11 (+ 15)

  12 + 13 + 14

  16 + 17 + 18 + 19 + 20

Logically, the 20 paragraphs in Text 11A should be only 5 paragraphs. These paragraphs can be joined because there is no change of time, place or topic between them. News reports tend to use shorter paragraphs than other genres of writing because they are purely informative and information is more easily assimilated if it is broken up for the reader. Newspapers rely on sales achieved through the accessibility of their layout for people who have a limited attention span, or who do not have the time or ability to wade through dense text, so their pages must have 'white space'. Because sub-editors cut news reports from the bottom upwards if they are too long for the space available, the information is given in descending order of importance.

**5** Texts 11B–D: headlines:

'Boy killed by crocodile'; 'Crocodile George spends six nights up a tree'; 'Monster crocs dined on dinosaurs'

The headlines are the briefest possible summaries of the report to follow. This is partly because of space limitations for newpaper headlines, but also because their aim is to arouse shock, horror and curiosity to make the reader go on to read the report to get the rest of the information. Headlines use the present tense for immediacy and space saving, unless the event took place in the distant past, as in Text 11D. The third headline contains assonance (*Monster croc* and *dined on dinosaurs*), alliteration (*dined on dinosaurs*) and abbreviation (*croc*), and in these aspects it is typical of the language of headlines.

**6** Texts 11B–D: summary points: [21 points]

**a** Present-day crocodiles:
- eat children and puppies
- attract tourism
- live in mangrove swamps in Australia
- the number in the region has grown since 1971
- man-eaters can be legally killed, but may be transported elsewhere instead
- saltwater crocodiles are called 'salties'
- wait for prey at the bottom of trees
- their eyes seem red at night
- are opportunistic predators
- can sense injured prey
- live on fish and turtles
- African crocodiles drag land animals into water where they drown and devour them

**b** Pre-historic crocodiles:
- were the major predator in Africa 110 million years ago
- used to eat dinosaurs
- had skulls 2 metres long
- had jaws with more than 100 teeth
- had more penetrating teeth than modern crocodiles
- probably attacked land animals at waterholes after hiding under water
- are now called *Sarcosuchus Imperator* ('flesh crocodile emperor')
- were first discovered by French scientists in 1964
- did not mature until at least 50 years of age

**8** Text 11B: complex sentence:

A five-year old boy in Queensland, who was last seen 12 days ago when playing with his brother near his home, was eaten by a crocodile while trying to protect his puppy.

News reports favour simple or compound sentences for dramatic effect and simplicity of expression, as befits informative writing for a mass readership. Summary style benefits from the use of complex sentence structures because they allow several points to be amalgamated into one sentence, making expression more concise and reducing the danger of overlong responses.

**9** Text 11C: news bulletin:

Queensland cattle rancher David George, 53, has spent a week up a tree looking down into the jaws of two hungry crocodiles. He stumbled into a swamp crawling with the reptiles after falling from his horse. Surrounded by saltwater crocodiles and injured, Mr George was forced to climb a tree, where he spent six nights tied to a branch. Having survived by drinking moisture from leaves, he was finally rescued by helicopter after being spotted sending distress signals.

**11** Text 11E: half-page summary:

Divers are viewed as other predators by sharks, not as prey or providers of food. Very few shark species of the many hundreds are dangerous, and even those which are a threat are rarely seen and cause few deaths. Sharks do not attack without warning or reason, the most common one being mistaken identity for an injured seal. When moving slowly and gracefully, sharks are not likely to be planning an attack, so divers are safe even without additional protection, provided that they are not trying to entice the sharks with fish blood, in which case they should be in a cage.

# Summary

## Unit 12 Caught in the web

### Topic outline

- **Syllabus component:** Paper 2 question 3; Paper 3 section 1; Paper 4 assignment 3; Paper 6 task 3
- **Main skills:** summary
- **Secondary skills:** discussion; selecting material; argument style; discursive writing
- **Outcome:** summary; *argument analysis; *argument dialogue; school magazine article
- **Materials:** speeches for and against the Internet
- **Texts:** Text 12A: Speech in favour; Text 12B: Speech against

### Lesson plan

1. Ask students for their opinion on the role of the Internet. Elicit both positive and negative views. (5)

2. Ask students to skim-read Text 12A. (5)

3. Ask students to re-read Text 12A in small groups and decide how to reduce it to half its length, i.e. five paragraphs, without losing anything essential. Go around the class listening to the quality of the arguments and level of participation (you may wish to assess the group discussions for Paper 6 task 3). (10)

4. Invite feedback from group representatives on decisions and justifications. (5)

5. Ask students, in pairs, to select points from the reduced Text 12A which argue for the benefits of the Internet. (5)

6. Collect a list of points on the board and ask students to make a copy. (5)

7. Read out Text 12B while students listen and make notes of the points being presented. (5)

8. Ask students to read Text 12B themselves and confirm whether they selected all the relevant points. (5)

9. Ask students, in pairs, to study the style and punctuation of Text 12B and identify the features of argumentative speech. (5)

10. Elicit features and examples of argumentative style. List them on board and discuss their persuasive effect. (5)

11. Invite suggestions for new titles for Texts 12A and 12B which summarise their content (perhaps a phrase from the text). Vote on the best title for each. (5)

12. Ask students to plan and write an answer to the following task, using Texts 12A and 12B and their notes: Summarise a) the benefits and b) the dangers of the existence of the Internet both now and in the future. Tell students to mention at least 15 relevant points, to use their own words, and to write no more than one page of average-sized writing. (25)

13. Ask students to check their summaries against the success criteria for Paper 2 Question 3: summary writing (see Success criteria document on CD-ROM). Collect summaries to assess (15 marks for content, 5 for style). (5)

### Homework task

Analyse the persuasive devices and evaluate the quality of the arguments used in Text 12B. (10)

### Additional tasks

a. Ask students to script and perform an argument between two students, one of whom is passionately in favour of and one strongly opposed to the way the Internet has changed our lives.

b. Ask students to write a school magazine article on the Internet's role in their education.

# Text 12A

# Speech in favour of Web 2.0

It can be argued that nothing has transformed day-to-day life in the 21st century as much as the arrival of the Internet. Throughout the developed world, and increasingly in the developing world as well, individuals take it for granted that they can 'go online' and within seconds find the answers to questions or communicate instantly with people worldwide whom they have in all probability never met.

The Internet is a social phenomenon all the more fascinating because it was never actually planned; it simply 'grew', with a minimum of direction or control, and the explosion in its use has left authorities struggling to cope with the increasingly complex social and political implications.

The origins of the Internet lie deep in the Cold War. Many American scientists and military leaders feared a surprise Soviet nuclear strike which would, among many other consequences, destroy the vulnerable communications upon which military command depended. A group of scientists at the Defense Advanced Research Projects Agency took advantage of recent developments in computer technology to come up with the idea of a distributed network with multiple routes for information to travel – every computer linked to every other by humble telephone lines, able to access each other's data. Because there were millions of telephone lines, the data would always find a way through. This principle, applied worldwide to millions of computers, still underlies the Internet today.

As is now the stuff of legend, the transformation of the private DARPANET into the public Internet was the brainchild of a brilliant English scientist working at the CERN research lab in Geneva, Switzerland, Tim Berners-Lee, who invented the name 'World Wide Web', and crucially invented the idea of the 'URL' – the Uniform Resource Locator – which is a kind of giant, invisible phone book which enables users to type in a simple address such as 'www.cnn.com'. The computer converts this into a 'real' electronic address, and routes the data through any available channel in milliseconds.

Initial interest in the Internet centred around three areas: finding information quickly, communicating via email, and, for young people especially, 'talking' to unknown like-minded strangers in 'chat-rooms'. But as the users and technology matured, new emphases began to emerge, and the coining of the phrase 'Web 2.0' to describe this phenomenon in 2004 by Tim O'Reilly initiated general public discussion of these trends.

The very phrase 'Web 2.0' is itself Internet-speak: new versions of software are given numbers, and minor changes are given numbers after the decimal point; so 2.0 means 'second generation', with the expectation that it will soon be updated to Web 2.1, Web 2.2 and so on until the third generation comes along. It is misleading, though, because it describes neither a new technology nor something developed by any individual; it is rather a way of summarising important changes in emphasis which are emerging as Internet users become more sophisticated, capable and widespread.

The key to the transformation to Web 2.0 is, again, technological development. In the Web 1.0 era, the software used to create web pages – based on the original 'Hyper Text Markup Language' (HTML) – was so complex that only 'geeks' (technical specialists) could use it, with the consequence that they also controlled page content. Now, anyone can create a web page or a web-log ('blog'), upload photos or post videos on the web. Web 2.0 is a democratic web; it is the people's web. For example, traditional reference sources have been supplanted by collaborative ventures such as Wikipedia, a free online encyclopaedia to which anyone can contribute articles or change them. One of the ten most-visited sites on the Internet, it now has 6 million entries in 249 languages and is visited by 280,000 people worldwide every minute of every day.

The other change which has enabled Web 2.0 to take off is the mass availability of broadband connections, at least in the developed world. In the early days of dial-up connections, a single image could take up to a minute to download or upload, and the idea of watching 'streaming video' was for most people a joke. Now, with new connection technologies, including 'permanently on' broadband connections, large files can be handled in seconds. It is the visual content of the web which really makes it different from the telephone; a digital photograph or video clip, taken on a camera phone of the kind which millions of people carry, can be emailed or on a website within seconds. Wireless connections ('Wi-Fi') and Bluetooth are also liberating people from the need to find a connection to plug into in order to get online.

Everyone who wants it can now have their own personal website on one of the dozens of 'social' sites which have been created: examples are MySpace, Bebo and Flickr. It takes just a few clicks to enter your personal details (true or fictionalised), upload a few photos, link to the profiles of some 'friends' and join the great global social community. Nor is this freedom restricted to the young, although they constitute a huge proportion of web users; many people have taken to the web in their retirement and are known as 'silver surfers'.

So what comes next? One thing that is certain is that the fast-moving world of the Internet will be hard to predict. Perhaps people will tire of viewing low-quality video clips of trivia, or the novelty of having one's own website may wear off. There may be a reaction against the superficiality and artificiality of pretending to conduct a 'social life' from your bedroom with people you can never meet in person. The pendulum may swing, and there may again arise a thirst for reliable information, rather than the opinions of unqualified bloggers. It is likely that governments will intervene (as they already do in many countries) to monitor the communications of individuals and to censor websites. Part of the joy of web-watching is seeing how this child of infinite potential grows as we watch it.

# Text 12B

# Speech against Web 2.0

'The Internet should be banned': there is a headline to catch the reader's attention. Surely everybody believes that the web has redefined social life, that it IS the future? No, not everybody; and it is not only repressive governments which think that the unlimited and instant global communication nexus is a very mixed blessing indeed.

One area of rapid growth in recent years has been in so-called 'social sites', where anyone can easily (and without cost) publish their own web page with personal photos, and provide an opportunity for their 'friends' to leave messages. This has created an unprecedented opening for cruel bullying, especially among the teenagers (and pre-teens) who constitute a huge proportion of those with pages on sites such as Facebook. The bullying is anonymous – although the victim is not – and there is no censorship, so there are no limits to the viciousness of the attacks. Even if the site is deleted and replaced by a new one, the bullies can find it in seconds. School counsellors have been inundated with cases of profoundly depressed teenagers, and the first cases of suicide have been reported. This 'cyber-bullying' is a wholly new phenomenon which could never have existed before social websites.

An arguably more fundamental issue concerns information and opinion forming. In most countries, the broadcast media are reasonably responsible, have to adhere to a code of conduct, and are overseen by watchdogs. They have to maintain at least a degree of impartiality. Laws of libel and slander protect reputations and deter the media from publishing unsubstantiated rumours. None of these restrictions apply in practice, however, to the Internet. No-one does or can censor what appears on individual websites; many are hosted in countries where there is no policing of content. The craze for 'blogging' (web-logging), where individuals write their thoughts about anything and everything, might be thought to be harmless – and indeed no-one has to read them – but in practice some build up huge followings and their writings are politically influential. Some would describe this as democracy at work, but it may be that many people prefer to have their prejudices reinforced; it is now illegal in civilised countries to preach racism, for example, but plenty of blogs do so.

One of the greatest threats facing the world today is that of global terrorism. The Internet and email make it possible for conspirators to communicate instantly with one another, at any time, wherever they are in the world; and, possibly, without being detected. There is a real danger of mathematically competent terrorists with advanced digital encryption technology planning global atrocities with impunity if they can keep one step ahead of the intelligence agencies who attempt to monitor them. There are now online tutorials for bomb-making.

Email has revolutionised communication, but it too has huge dangers. 'Spam' mail is more than a minor irritant; the time wasted in deleting it costs billions every day, and much of its content is offensive. Even if the USA – the source of more than 90% of 'spam' – were to ban it, the spammers would simply move their operations elsewhere. But there are other issues: the decline of literacy because it is considered acceptable to write even formal emails in a debased language with copious abbreviations and symbols; the fact that the tone of an email is misinterpreted by the recipient more than half the time. Instant communication is miscommunication.

There is also a significant threat to the academic world. Now that huge quantities of prepared essays are available on the Internet (at a price, for this is a very profitable business) students at every level, from GCSE coursework to university dissertations, are able to purchase work they could not have written. In the process they gain academic qualifications to which they are not entitled, and the social consequences are very worrying. There is no foolproof way of detecting plagiarism of this kind.

So much of the world now depends on computers and networked systems that we are much more vulnerable than previously to malicious attack from enemies who can damage our society without leaving their bedroom. Every country has a massive 'cyber warfare' department seeking ways of destroying an enemy's infrastructure. The Internet makes it possible for outsiders to gain access to the most critical of systems which run power stations and communications, and which manage air traffic control. 'Denial of Service' attacks have already crippled some of the most powerful corporations on the planet.

Furthermore, there are the morally corrosive effects of the unlimited availability to everyone (including children) of pornography and violence on the Internet; such images will inevitably desensitise their viewers and arguably lead to more extreme atrocities. The web endangers privacy, scholarship, security and morality. Until it can be properly policed, the web is a powerful weapon for criminals of all kinds, and it should be taken away from them to protect the rest of us.

# Answers – Unit 12

**3** Text 12A: reduction:

Paragraphs 1, 3, 4, 6 and 9 can be removed without losing any of the essential points the speech is making.

**5** Text 12A: summary points (from paragraphs 2, 5, 7, 8 and 10): [7 points]
- one can find information quickly
- one can communicate quickly
- one can meet new people in chat-rooms
- anyone can create a web page or blog
- broadband connection has now improved the services
- photos and video material can be quickly posted
- wireless connection has made Internet more accessible

**7** Text 12B: summary points: [16 points]
- social sites encourage bullying, which may lead to suicide
- rumours cannot be prevented
- no policing of content
- bloggers with prejudices have political influence
- false information quickly spreads around the world
- global terrorism made possible through communication of conspirators
- spam wastes billions of dollars of work time every day
- content of spam is often offensive
- emails debase the use of language
- tone of more than 50% of emails misinterpreted
- students can cheat and plagiarise to gain qualifications dishonestly
- hackers can get confidential information
- cyber warriors can destroy computer systems and damage society
- pornography and violent images are available to children
- violence desensitises and leads to more atrocities
- the Internet is a weapon for all kinds of criminal

**10** Text 12B: argumentative features and effects:

provocative title arouses interest and fury; rhetorical questions force reader to feel engaged; strong language, such as *bullying*, *viciousness*, evokes sympathy; triple structures are the most convincing form of persuasion; epigrammatic phrases, such as *instant communication is miscommunication*, are short, memorable sayings; paragraph openers give the impression of how many arguments there are to support the adopted view (*One of ...*, *And then there is ...*, *So much of ...*, *In the case of ...*, *There is also ...*); examples derived from life-threatening scenarios and threats of terminal dangers to society concentrate the reader's mind and arouse fear (e.g. references to terrorism, enemies, air-traffic control, criminals).

**11** Texts 12A and 12B: new titles:

**Text 12A**: 'Welcome to the web'; 'Transforming the world'; 'Finding a way through'; 'Like-minded strangers'; 'The people's web'; 'Permanently connected'; 'Gateway to freedom'; 'The great global community'; 'Cyber-space surfing'; 'The joy of web-watching'

**Text 12B**: 'Ban the Net!'; 'A very mixed blessing indeed'; 'No limits, no censorship'; 'Watchdogs without teeth'; 'People power gone mad?'; 'Keeping one step ahead?'; 'Unstoppable'; 'Crippling the corporations'; 'Morally corrosive'; 'Proper policing just a pipedream'; 'Web criminals rule, OK?'

# Directed writing

## Unit 13 Kept apart

### Topic outline

- **Syllabus component:** Paper 3 section 1; Paper 6 individual task
- **Main skills:** dialogue; speech writing
- **Secondary skills:** selecting material; adopting a voice; vocabulary building; developing material; collating material
- **Outcome:** dialogue Paper 6 task 2; informative speech Paper 6 task 1; argument speech; *debate speech; *formal letter
- **Materials:** magazine feature articles; exchange of letters
- **Texts:** Text 13A: Brothers at war; Text 13B: What Rosa did; Text 13C: Rosa Parks' letter

### Lesson plan

1 Choose two students to read out Text 13A in role. (5)

2 Ask students to highlight the key information about the experience of Luis and of Amaral during the time they were apart (i.e. after the abduction by Unita and before the reunion). (5)

3 Ask students to transfer the highlighted material, in their own words, to two columns. (5)

4 Ask students, in pairs, to write the dialogue between the brothers at their meeting after 29 years; they should explain what happened to them, how they felt then, and how they feel now about the war and their separation. (10)

5 Choose pairs to perform their dialogues. Vote on the best script in terms of content and voice. (10)

6 Ask students to read Text 13B and to underline unknown words. (5)

7 Ask students to guess the meanings of these words using the recommended methods (dividing words into constituent parts, family word connections, other language similarities, logical meaning within context). Write words and meanings on board. (5)

8 Ask students to scan Text 13B to identify and highlight relevant information for a speech about the life and achievement of Rosa Parks. (5)

9 Ask students to read Text 13C, highlighting any new information about Rosa Parks. (5)

10 Ask students to transfer the material from Texts 13B and 13C, in their own words, and arrange it in a plan in logical order. (5)

11 Ask students to write a funeral oration for Rosa Parks, who died in 2005, of about one page. They should consider V(oice), A(udience), R(egister), P(urpose) when choosing a style of writing. (15)

12 Choose students to read their speeches aloud (you may conduct a Speaking and Listening coursework assessment and give feedback). Collect speeches for assessment as a directed writing task (mark out of 15 for Writing and out of 10 for Reading). (15)

### Homework task

Write a speech to give in a school assembly on the theme of prejudice. Select, develop and integrate material from Texts 13A, 13B and 13C to explain the damaging effects of political and racial discrimination.

### Additional tasks

a Ask students, in pairs, to write a debate speech for or against the motion: 'This house believes that the use of child soldiers cannot ever be justified.' Hold the debate and take a vote according to the effectiveness of the speeches.

b Ask students, in small groups, to discuss and draft a letter to a person they admire, to ask them something about their beliefs and actions. (Some of these could be typed up and sent after being read to the class.)

© Cambridge University Press 2010

# Text 13A

# Brothers at war

LUIS: I was with my mum in the fields in November 1975 when my dad ran to tell her that the Portuguese were leaving Angola. Although our country was free of the Portuguese, there was then civil war between two factions – the MPLA and Unita. Like many people, my parents were caught in the middle. Now, from being people who worked hard and had good times, we became people who had little and were often on the run. Our lives were a nightmare.

In December 1976 tragedy struck. It was a Sunday in the Christmas holidays, when my brother was home. We were in church praying, and the choir was singing, when suddenly faces appeared at every window. It was MPLA soldiers who marched in and announced to the congregation: 'Everyone outside – but we only want the teenage boys.' Shocked and scared, everyone left the church and the soldiers seized six boys, including Amaral, who was 14. My father rushed to stop them, but the soldiers immediately set on him and beat him.

That night my brother managed to escape the soldiers and fled back to our village. Amaral and his friends hid for the next few days, but some nights later, as they sat in our kitchen planning what to do, we heard the terrible sound of soldiers' boots marching towards our house. This time it was the Unita soldiers, who didn't wear uniform. As they marched in, I was like a mouse, trying to hide in the corner. 'Don't beat me – just take me,' pleaded my brother. It was all over very quickly. I had to wake my parents and tell them my brother had been abducted a second time. I didn't see my brother again for 29 years.

As the days went on, I could see in my parents' faces an increasing sense of hopelessness. My father was frequently beaten by MPLA soldiers because my brother was serving in the Unita forces. I understood all too well that I could be taken too, and I was afraid all the time – especially at night. To be safe I'd often sleep with the cattle in the field. At night my mum used to make a fire with green leaves underneath, a traditional invocation. As it burnt she'd call 'Amaral, come back!' But he didn't. At school the teachers would say: 'You, boy, does your brother come to see your parents at night?' One teacher made me kneel on a pile of small stones, trying to get information out of me about Unita. I knew nothing, but I still have the scars from the stones.

In 1981 I moved to a small town to continue my studies. But when I was 15, the inevitable happened – I was abducted by the MPLA, on my way to school. I was a soldier until 1992, and it was a very hard life. As a soldier you have to be bad and kill people. I soon became a tank-company commander on the front line. But in 1990 our brigade was completely destroyed by Unita. All around me I saw people dying like animals, all covered in blood. What I didn't know was that my brother was also on the front line – on the other side. We may even have fought each other.

In early 1992 I was demobilised. When my brother didn't reappear we had to accept he was dead, so we held a funeral for him. We didn't know that he was in a refugee camp in Zambia. One day my father received a letter from him through the International Red Cross. I'll never forget the day we were reunited. I walked into my sister's house in Huambo. There were my sisters, my father, and a man with a mutilated leg. I couldn't speak. We embraced each other. Over a big lunch we tried to tell each other our stories.

AMARAL: I left Luis when he was only four years old, when I was abducted. Because of the civil war the two opposing political parties wanted young people who were able to read and write to serve in their armies. The first time I was abducted I managed to escape and went back to the village, but a few nights later I was abducted again with three friends by Unita soldiers. I didn't cry, but I was frightened because I didn't know where they were taking me. On the way to the camp we had to climb mountains and cross rivers and I was afraid I'd be killed.

At the camp there were six other boys the same age as me, but Unita did not have enough weapons for us, so we were given sticks and taught to ambush MPLA soldiers. If we had not done what we were told, the commander would have shot us. I was always thinking about running away but I was too scared. And then I stepped on a land mine and lost my leg. As things got worse and our fellow soldiers were dying around us in very bloody battles, we developed anger and wanted revenge against the MPLA soldiers. But all of us were black, and we could not understand why we were killing each other.

During our 29-year separation I prayed that I would see my brother again. I missed him a lot. I left him as a child and I could only try to imagine how he was growing up. I never thought that I would find him so well educated. When we met at my sister's house we were surprised and nobody spoke. I had not expected that my brother and I would ever meet again, and soon I was crying. I had been worried how it would be, because I had been Unita and Luis had been MPLA. But when we talked about it we didn't have any anger, because we were forced to do what we did.

Adapted from *Sunday Times*, 24th February 2008.

# Text 13B

# What Rosa did

It is a familiar story. It was at about 6 p.m. on 1st December 1955 that 42-year-old department store worker Rosa Parks boarded a bus in Montgomery, Alabama, USA, to ride home after a day at work. In those days buses in the southern USA were racially segregated: the first four rows of seats were reserved for white passengers. Having bought her ticket, she walked past these 'whites-only' rows and chose to sit in the first row of seats for 'coloured' people like herself. As Parks herself commented later, it seemed to be an ordinary day.

But as the bus filled up, it became apparent to the driver that there were too many white passengers for the four reserved rows, so he asked those sitting in Parks' row to move back and give their seats to white passengers. Some of the 'coloured' people obeyed, but Rosa decided not to move. 'If you need to arrest me then you may,' she politely told the driver. It was not that she was feeling especially tired after her day at work. Many years later, looking back on that day, Rosa Parks observed 'I was not tired physically, or no more tired than I usually was at the end of a working day. The only tired I was, was tired of giving in.'

She was arrested by the police and fined for her act of defiance. But her refusal to comply with a racist order on that day was to change history and lead to the end of racial segregation in America.

Rosa Parks was born in 1913, when slavery was a living memory for her grandparents and it was impossible even to imagine real equality before the law for African Americans. She developed a keen sense of social justice early in her life, and when she married Raymond Parks in 1932 at the age of 20 she became actively involved in the emerging civil rights movement. Her husband encouraged Rosa to be politically active, and he made sure she was on the voters' register at a time when this was rare for African Americans. At this time, although racial segregation had been outlawed by the federal government, it remained an intrusive fact of life in most southern states, like Alabama, where parts of buses and public places were reserved for whites.

Rosa Parks' unplanned act of defiance proved to be timely. A softly spoken model citizen, she was easy to cast in the role of wronged victim, eliciting sympathy worldwide and contributing to a coalition of opposition to the humiliation of segregation.

Just one day after her arrest, the black community in Montgomery swung into action. It organised a state-wide boycott of the bus system which was planned to last for one day but ended up running for 380 days. Encouraged by the success of this boycott, an association was formed to fight the whole system of segregation; a prominent member was the young and then-unknown Dr Martin Luther King. It turned Parks' individual act of courage into a nationwide social and political campaign. Segregation on buses ended, and full legal equality was achieved not long after.

Although Parks travelled around America to speak about her experiences, she mostly preferred a life out of the spotlight. Arguably one of the best-known women in the civil rights movement, she nevertheless continued to work as a seamstress. Over the years, she received many awards and accolades; perhaps the most moving was when Nelson Mandela, recently freed from prison, said that Rosa Parks and her story had been an inspiration to him throughout his 27 years of imprisonment.

Rosa Parks changed the world through a single act of principled determination, but that had not been her intention at the time. 'I did not get on the bus to get arrested,' she said. 'I got on the bus to go home.'

# Text 13C

# Letters to and from Rosa Parks

Dear Mrs Parks,

The sixth graders are doing a history project. We chose you. The theme is 'Taking a stand in history'. We have some questions. Can you answer them? How did you feel when you were on the bus? Have you had any experiences with the Ku Klux Klan?

********

Dear Sixth Graders,

Your theme is a good one. A person should not take a stand to make history. Taking a stand for what is right is most important. You may take a stand to make history, and it can be the wrong one. So many people did this during the Civil Rights movement, and many are still doing it today.

The custom of getting on the bus for black people in Montgomery in the 1950s was to pay at the front door, get off the bus, and then re-enter through the back door to find a seat. Black people could not sit in the same rows with white people. This custom was humiliating and intolerable.

When I sat down on the bus on the day I was arrested, I decided I must do what was right to do. People have said over the years that the reason I did not give up my seat was because I was tired. I did not think of being physically tired. My feet were not hurting. I was tired in a different way. I was tired of seeing so many men treated as boys and not called by their proper names or titles. I was tired of seeing children and women mistreated and disrespected because of the color of their skin. I was tired of Jim Crow laws, of legally enforced racial segregation.

I thought of the pain and the years of oppression and mistreatment that my people had suffered. I felt that way every day. December 1, 1955, was no different. Fear was the last thing I thought of that day. I put my trust in the Lord for guidance and help to endure whatever I had to face. I knew I was sitting in the right seat.

I did experience the Ku Klux Klan when I was young. I remember being about six years old and hearing about how the KKK terrorized African Americans by burning down their churches and beating up or even killing people. My family talked about wearing our clothes to bed so we would be ready to escape our house if we had to.

My grandfather never seemed afraid. He was a proud man who believed in protecting his home. When the hate crimes escalated, he sat up many nights with his shotgun. He said if the KKK broke into our house, he was going to get the first one who came through the door. The Klansmen never did try to break into our house, but their violence continued. After these experiences, I learned that I must not be afraid and must always trust in God.

I hope you and your classmates never experience hateful violence. By learning about the past, you are already helping a great deal toward making the future better for people of all races.

**Jim Crow laws** – USA state laws enacted between 1876 and 1965 which mandated segregation between black and white Americans in all public facilities.

**Ku Klux Klan** – Ku Klux Klan (KKK, from Greek 'kyklos' meaning 'circle') is the name of organisations in the United States that have advocated white supremacy, racism, anti-Semitism, anti-Catholicism, homophobia, anti-Communism and nativism. These organisations have used terrorism, violence and acts of intimidation, such as cross burning (a symbol of going to war) and lynching, to oppress African Americans and other social or ethnic groups. There were 6 million estimated members in 1924, and even nowadays, when membership is illegal, they are thought to be in the region of 6000.

Source: *Dear Mrs Parks – A Dialogue with Today's Youth* by Rosa Parks, Lee & Low Books, 1997.

# Answers – Unit 13

2  Text 13A: main points:

   a  Luis' experiences:
   - watched parents lose hope
   - father beaten by MPLA soldiers
   - so afraid of being abducted he slept (with the cattle) in the field
   - mother lit fires to call for Amaral to return
   - tortured by MPLA supporters for infomation about Unita
   - transferred to another school in town
   - abducted by MPLA on way to school aged 15
   - became tank-company commander and sent to front line
   - brigade destroyed by Unita in 1990 and many killed
   - demobilised in 1992
   - assumed Amaral was dead so funeral was held
   - received letter from Amaral through the International Red Cross

   b  Amaral's experiences:
   - frightened by the journey to the camp with three friends
   - with six other boys in camp, the same age of 14
   - they were given sticks instead of weapons
   - too scared to disobey or run away
   - had a leg blown off by a mine
   - developed a hatred for the MPLA
   - couldn't understand why blacks were killing each other
   - missed his baby brother and didn't expect to see him again
   - worried by the meeting after 29 years because they'd been on opposing sides

10  Texts 13B and 13C: points about the life and achievement of Rosa Parks:
   - born in 1913
   - maternal grandparents instilled a sense of social justice
   - she married Raymond Parks in 1932 at the age of 20
   - her husband encouraged her to be politically active
   - although racial segregation was officially outlawed, Alabama still allowed it
   - she was softly spoken and a model citizen
   - bus incident 1st December 1955 in Montgomery, Alabama
   - then a 42-year-old department-store worker
   - refused to move when asked to free up seating for white passengers
   - she was tired of giving in and told the driver to arrest her
   - she was arrested and fined
   - the local coloured community supported her action
   - 40,000 African Americans supported a boycott of the Montgomery bus system
   - the campaign lasted just over a year
   - Dr Martin Luther King became involved
   - legal equality was finally granted
   - she gave some talks about her experience
   - she continued a quiet life working as a seamstress
   - she was praised by many leading political figures in her later life, including Nelson Mandela
   - her action set in motion a series of events which led to the abolition of racial segregation
   - she changed the world by her simple and unplanned act of defiance

# Directed writing

## Unit 14 Native speakers

**Topic outline**

- **Syllabus component:** Paper 3 section 1; Paper 2 question 3; Paper 6 paired task
- **Main skills:** selecting material; structuring material; genre transformation
- **Secondary skills:** vocabulary building; developing material; collating material; discursive writing
- **Outcome:** directed writing; dialogue; formal letter; *summary; *magazine article
- **Materials:** personal and informative passages; formal letter structure handout
- **Texts:** Text 14A: Good for business; Text 14B: India calling

## Lesson plan

1. Ask students to suggest difficulties which a family emigrating to a country with a different language and culture would face. (5)

2. Ask students to read Text 14A. (5)

3. Ask students for synonyms for the ten words in bold. (5)

4. Ask students, in pairs, to re-read Text 14A and highlight evidence (in different colours) of a) the attitude of the father to living in America, b) the attitude of the father to the son, c) the attitude of the son to living in America, and d) the attitude of the son to the father. (10)

5. Ask students to structure the highlighted material in a plan, then write a letter of reminiscence to the son from the father in his hospital bed. They should adapt the material to suit the change of voice, audience and time perspective. (25)

6. Ask students to check the content, style and accuracy of their writing. Collect responses to assess as directed writing tasks (15 marks for voice, audience and style, including range of vocabulary and sentence structures; 10 marks for content including inference, development, use of detail – see the Paper 3 mark scheme on the CIE Teacher Support website). (5)

7. Ask students to skim-read Text 14B. (5)

8. Ask students to scan Text 14B to select and highlight the emotional and physical problems caused by working in a call centre. (10)

9. Ask students, in pairs, to script a dialogue between an Indian who works in a call centre in New Delhi and her/his cousin who emigrated to America a few months ago, using the material from both passages to provide a balanced conversation about their working lives and the difficulties they are facing. (10)

10. Invite pairs to perform their dialogues. Evaluate the selection, development and integration of material. (10)

## Homework task

Use the material you collected for task 8 to plan and write a formal letter (see CD-ROM for formal letter structure handout) of about a side and a half from a call-centre employee to his/her boss, describing symptoms and asking for something to be done to improve working conditions.

## Additional tasks

a   Ask students to use the material they collected in task 4 to write a response to the summary questions: a) What did the writer feel about his father and the way he adapted to life in New York? b) What did the writer's father feel about his son and the way he responded to life in New York?

b   Ask students to plan and write a language magazine article entitled 'Another language: another life', which collates the material from Texts 14A and 14B and discusses the effects on people who have to change their language because of emigration or employment.

**Text 14A**

# Good for business

*Korean-American Henry Park reminisces about his father, who has just had a stroke and is in hospital in New York.*

I thought his life was all about money. He drew much energy and pride from his ability to make it almost at will. He was some kind of human annuity. He had no real cleverness or secrets for good business; he simply refused to fail, leaving absolutely nothing to luck or chance or someone else. Of course, in his personal **lore** he would have said that he started with $200 in his pocket and a wife and baby and just a few words of English. Knowing what every native loves to hear, he would have offered the classic immigrant story, **casting** himself as the heroic newcomer, self-sufficient, resourceful.

The truth, though, is that my father got his first **infusion** of capital from a ggeh, a Korean 'money club' in which members contributed to a pool that was given out on a rotating basis. Each week you gave the specified amount; and then one week in the cycle, all the money was yours. [...]

I know over the years my father and his friends got together less and less. Certainly, after my mother died, he didn't seem to want to go to the gatherings anymore. But it wasn't just him. They all got busier and wealthier and lived farther and farther apart. Like us, their families moved to big houses with big yards to **tend** on weekends, and they owned fancy cars that needed washing and waxing. They joined their own neighborhood pool and tennis clubs and were making drinking friends with Americans. Some of them, too, were already dead, like Mr. Oh, who had a heart attack after being held up at his store in Hell's Kitchen. And in the end my father no longer belonged to any ggeh; he complained about all the disgraceful troubles that were now **cropping up**, people not paying on time or leaving too soon after their turn of getting the money. In America, he said, it's even hard to stay Korean.

I wonder if my father, if given the chance, would have wished to go back to the time before he made all that money, when he had just one store and we rented a tiny apartment in Queens. He worked hard and had worries but he had a joy then that he never seemed to regain once the money started coming in. He might turn on the radio and dance cheek to cheek with my mother. He worked on his car himself, a used green Impala with carburetor trouble. They had lots of Korean friends that they met at church and then even in the street, and when they talked in public there was a shared sense of how lucky they were, to be in America but still have countrymen near. [...]

What belief did I ever hold in my father, whose daily life I so often ridiculed and looked upon with such **abject** shame? The summer before I started high school he made me go with him to one of the new stores on Sunday afternoons to help restock the shelves and the bins. I hated going. My friends – suddenly including some girls – were always playing tennis or going to the pool club then. I never gave the reason why I always declined, and they eventually stopped asking. Later I found out from one of them, my first girlfriend, that they simply thought I was religious. When I was working for him I wore a white apron over my slacks and dress shirt and tie. The store was on Madison Avenue in the Eighties and my father made all the employees dress up for the blue-haired matrons, and the fancy dogs, and the sensible young mothers pushing antique velvet-draped prams, and their most quiet of infants, and the banker fathers **brooding** about, annoyed and **aloof** and humorless.

My father, thinking that it might be good for business, urged me to show them how well I spoke English, to make a display of it, to casually recite 'some Shakespeare words'. [...] Mostly, though, I threw all my frustration into building those perfect pyramids of fruit. The other two workers seemed to have even more bottled up inside them, their worries of money and family. They marched through the work of the store as if they wanted to **deplete** themselves of every last bit of energy, every means and source of struggle. They peeled and sorted and bunched and sprayed and cleaned and stacked and shelved and swept; my father put them to anything for which they didn't have to speak. They both had college degrees and knew no one in the country and spoke little English. The men, whom I knew as Mr. Yoon and Mr. Kim, were both recent immigrants in their thirties with wives and young children. They worked twelve-hour days six days a week for $200 cash and meals and all the fruit and vegetables we couldn't or wouldn't sell; it was the typical arrangement. My father, like all successful immigrants before him, gently and not so gently exploited his own. 'This is way I learn business; this is way they learn business.'

And although I knew he gave them a $100 bonus every now and then I never let on that I felt he was anything but cruel to his workers. I still imagine Mr. Kim's and Mr. Yoon's children, lonely for their fathers, gratefully eating whatever was brought home to them, our overripe and almost rotten mangoes, our papayas, kiwis, pineapples, these **exotic** tastes of their wondrous new country, this joyful fruit now too soft and too sweet for those who knew better, us near natives, us earlier Americans.

**Source:** *Native Speaker* by Chang-Rae Lee, Penguin, 1996.

**Note:** American spelling used throughout.

# Text 14B

# INDIA CALLING

It seemed such a simple and profitable business idea. Transferring call centres from Britain to English-speaking India would save billions of pounds for big business. Many high-street names, keen to slash up to 40% off their labour costs, have rushed to 'offshore' their call centres. Forecasters predict that, in the near future, the Indian call-centre boom will be worth 6 billion pounds.

However, in their rush for profit, Western companies are failing to take into account the human fallout of this lucrative shift. Recently, a massive upsurge in mental-health problems is being reported by Indian workers struggling to cope with the complex demands of dealing with a different culture down a phone line and high staff burnout rates are becoming a problem. The crux of the problem lies with identity. Indian employees are trained to neutralise their accents and disguise their nationality by adopting Western names; they are also forced to work through the night to fit in with UK and US business hours. New research suggests that depression, identity confusion and even drug abuse are now emerging as side-effects of the job, along with sleep-related disorders and relationship difficulties.

Dr Sanjay Chugh, chairman of the International Institute of Mental Health in Delhi, says he has seen more than 250 patients whose problems stem directly from call-centre jobs. Most Indians get pre-job instruction in subjects such as listening skills and telesales etiquette. Some are given a crash course in British culture. But learning about the Brits' love of fish and chips and the nation's passion for football doesn't come near to equipping them for the stresses they will face. 'A lot of clients complain about problems around having to switch their identities completely twice a day,' says Dr Chugh. 'They also find themselves getting subjected to a huge amount of emotional and verbal abuse.'

After doing the night shift in an Indian call centre, trying to survive on four hours' sleep a day, call-centre worker Laksmi, 40, found she began to suffer confusion which she likens to jetlag. 'I would wake up thinking, is this the middle of the week? Do I have to get up?' She also found the tedium hard to handle. 'We had to stick to the script. We were programmed. It was so monotonous, I found myself saying it in my sleep.'

According to new research by psychiatrist Dr Raj Persaud, who travelled to the subcontinent to examine the situation, the only way Indians will learn to cope with psychological pressure of this kind is to adopt a more Western approach. Apparently, in the UK we are more used to compartmentalising our lives and being polite to people when working, even when we don't feel like it. But in countries such as India this isn't the case and this 'emotional labour' is taking its toll.

'There are two types of protective role-play common in the West,' explains Dr Persaud, 'superficial acting, which is the kind you get when a shop assistant tells you to "Have a nice day"; it's insincere but part of the performance of being polite. And then there's deep acting, which is getting fully immersed in the role – like an actor does.' Dr Persaud argues that deep-acting techniques can protect workers psychologically, but these changes in behaviour come at a cost. 'It seems you have to import a bit of Western culture into your company. You have to ask, does this process begin to contaminate your culture? And is that something you want?'

Source: Jane Cassidy, *Independent on Sunday*, 20th February 2005.

# Answers – Unit 14

**3** Text 14A: synonyms:

**lore** – *legend, tradition*
**casting** – *allocating a theatrical role*
**infusion** – *insertion, introduction*
**tend** – *care for, cultivate*
**cropping up** – *appearing occasionally*

**abject** – *hopeless, helpless*
**brooding** – *preoccupied with sombre thoughts*
**aloof** – *apart, distant, detached, reserved*
**deplete** – *empty, drain, exhaust*
**exotic** – *foreign, unusual, strange*

**4** Text 14A: attitudes:

**a** Father's attitude to living in America
- proud of being able to make money
- refused to fail or leave anything to chance
- saw himself as the classic immigrant who started poor but independently became rich
- actually relied on financial support from Korean community
- became reclusive and disillusioned with his compatriots
- became busier and wealthier as time passed
- became more integrated into local society
- was strict with his employees

**b** Father's attitude to son:
- believed his son should work in his shops rather than have American friends
- used him to show off to well-to-do customers
- thought he should be made to work as hard as his other employees
- believed that he should learn the hard way to be a successful businessman

**c** Son's attitude to living in America:
- resented having to work in the shop on Sunday afternoons
- was too ashamed of his father to explain to his peers why he had to decline their social invitations
- channelled his frustration into displaying the fruit in his father's shop
- felt sorry for the recent immigrants and their lonely children

**d** Son's attitude to father:
- thought his father only cared about money
- wondered whether wealth spoilt his father and his ability to feel joy
- regretted that his father lost his Korean friends
- rejected his father's beliefs and felt ashamed of him
- gave impression he believed his father was too harsh with his Korean employees
- thought that his father exploited his fellow immigrants

**8** Text 14B: problems arising from working in a call centre:

**a** Emotional:
- mental-health problems
- high burnout rates
- identity crises
- depression
- relationship difficulties
- being subject to abuse on the phone
- tediousness of repeating script
- psychological pressure
- culture contamination

**b** Physical:
- working overseas business hours
- drug abuse
- sleep disorders
- stress
- lack of sleep
- confusion similar to jetlag

# Directed writing

## Unit 15 Dedicated and determined

**Topic outline**

- **Syllabus component:** Paper 3 question 1; Paper 2 question 1; Paper 6 task 2
- **Main skills:** genre transformation; persuasive writing
- **Secondary skills:** selecting material, developing material; evaluating material; summarising material
- **Outcome:** summary; descriptive account; formal report; persuasive speech; *dialogue; *appeal letter
- **Materials:** newspaper articles; formal report structure handout
- **Texts:** Text 15A: Medical aid; Text 15B: Academic aid

## Lesson plan

1 Choose students to read out Text 15A in turn. (5)

2 Ask students to re-read Text 15A to identify and collect material to write two paragraphs, one to summarise what Panupong does and the other to summarise why he does it. (15)

3 Invite students to read their paragraphs. Discuss whether they contain the relevant information. (5)

4 Ask students to read Text 15B. Ask them which text they think evokes more admiration and sympathy, and why. (5)

5 Ask students to re-read Text 15B, identifying and listing information about a typical day in Babur's life. (5)

6 Ask students to imagine they are Babur and to write a first-person account of a typical day in his life – called 'My school day' – from waking up to going to bed, about one side long. This account, in their own words, should infer, develop and add details to elaborate on the original passage. (15)

7 Ask students to check through their work for errors. Collect responses to assess as directed writing. (5)

8 Assign half the students the role of Panupong, and the other half that of Babur. Ask them to prepare a speech of about three-quarters of a side describing what they are doing and why they need financial help to be able to continue doing it successfully. The speeches should include ideas inferred from the text. (15)

9 Invite students to deliver their speeches. Judge them according to their persuasiveness (assessment for Paper 6 task 1). (10)

10 Using Texts 15A and 15B, and ideas from the speeches given in task 9, plan an answer to the directed writing task: You are the president of an international charity which supports community aid, and you have been asked by Panupong and Babur for financial support. Write your report to your committee, explaining what each of the young men do, evaluating the two cases of financial need in detail, and recommending one of them for support from your charity. (See CD-ROM for formal report structure handout.) (10)

## Homework task

Write your report (one and a half sides) to the charity committee.

## Additional tasks

a Ask students to imagine that Panupong and Babur have met, and to write, in pairs, and perform the conversation they might have; they should include questions they ask each other, explanations of why they do what they do, and plans for the future.

b Ask students to write an appeal letter to residents of their local community to raise money for setting up a medical rescue service or a school. They should explain why such an initiative is needed, how it would benefit the community as a whole, and what the funds would be spent on.

# Text 15A

# Medical AID

Last year, Panupong Lapsathien from Bangkok in Thailand won a prize worth one million baht on a television game show. One month later, the 22-year-old had spent all the money – and it was far from enough.

For instead of buying a new car, Panupong bought an ambulance. It was an old van, newly equipped with emergency medical equipment. He switches on the lights and sirens and speeds off to help anyone who calls in an emergency, free of charge, for Panupong is a member of the volunteer rescue team of Vajira Hospital, founded in 1994. For six years he spent much of his time on his bicycle, roaming the streets of Bangkok to provide on-the-spot first aid to the injured and homeless. But then Panupong had to stop biking. He was pedalling at full speed to the scene of an accident when he lost control of the bike on a bend and his leg was so badly damaged that he could see the bone poking through the skin. Panupong spent two months in hospital, and his leg remained in a splint for another two months. He was no longer able to jump on his two-wheeled ambulance, though he would prefer to use his bicycle. 'Riding a bicycle is quicker to get to the scene, as the van is always stuck in a traffic jam. And of course it is much cheaper than driving, with petrol prices so high.'

His volunteering takes up his time from 9 p.m. to 6 a.m., and is unpaid. He lives on an allowance from his mother and his work as a part-time lecturer and guest speaker at some universities and organisations. But it's never enough, he admitted. 'I can't afford to volunteer every day, but if I don't go, I feel upset. I feel as if it's my responsibility, a lifetime commitment. What if one day there's a car crash and no one goes to help? What if someone's dying and your radio is switched off?'

Compared to some, the young volunteers may seem to live an extreme, hectic life. Many of them do not have the time for watching movies, partying or other leisure activities. Yet they say they feel fulfilled. 'When I do CPR and help someone start breathing again, I feel so proud. To save someone's life is the greatest honour for me,' says Panupong. 'It makes my life meaningful.' Every day there are stories of accidents and illnesses. Panupong and the team handle four to six cases a day. 'There are many out there who have to sleep in pain, soaked and cold in the rain, without any care and attention from state hospitals,' he said. 'Once I saw a homeless man with a badly injured arm, and I took him to the hospital and then we sped off to other cases. When we drove back to the area we saw the same guy, with the same wound, lying in the same place. Isn't he a human being like us, with a right to medical care? But it seems no one wants to help or get involved. I'm feeling discouraged as these issues are unlikely to be solved. I am just a volunteer, and can change nothing.'

But his enthusiasm, devotion and commitment have been recognised, and he has just been awarded the Best Youth of the Nation and Asian Award. He has also appeared in many magazines and TV programmes, sharing his experiences and his passion with others. He believes everyone should learn at least basic first aid techniques, to be ready in case of an emergency. 'Accidents can happen to anyone, and the bandages, cotton wool and antiseptic in your medicine chest might not be enough.'

# Academic AID

For his classmates the four o'clock bell means lessons are over, but for 16-year-old Babur Ali it is time to take off his uniform and start a new school day as probably the youngest headmaster in the world.

Since he was 11, Babur has been running his own school in a small village in West Bengal, passing on to the children of the poor families the knowledge he has acquired at his fee-paying school during the day. It began when children in his village of jute farmers started plaguing him with questions about what he learnt at the 1000 rupee (£12) a year school their parents could not afford. Five years later he is acknowledged by district education officials as 'headmaster' with ten volunteer teachers and 650 pupils desperate to learn.

The school began in the open air, but today it is housed in two bamboo, brick and tile huts, where children are rotated between indoor and outdoor lessons, often with 80 to a class. He rises at 5 a.m. for morning prayers, does household chores, then takes a bus to school in a village 5 kilometres away. From 10 a.m. to 4 p.m. he focuses on his own education, then he races back to his village to welcome his students at 5 p.m.

He teaches the state school curriculum – English, Bengali, History and Maths – until 8 p.m. and supervises his colleagues, mainly fellow pupils ranging from 16 to 19 years old. The schedule does not weary him: 'I never feel tired – in fact teaching gives me more strength.'

Babur's dream of official status for his school moved closer last week, when he was honoured for slashing illiteracy rates in his district by West Bengal's chief minister at a ceremony in Kolkata. His parents were bursting with pride. Babur has succeeded in attracting pupils to school where the West Bengal authorities, the central government and international aid agencies have all failed. At Babur's school the teachers work unpaid, the children wear their own clothes and the books and desks are financed through donations.

Babur believes he has found his vocation. He wants to qualify as a teacher so that he can develop his school and educate more poor children. His plan is to enrol for an open university degree so that he will be able to do so without deserting his pupils. The secret of his success, he said, is commitment. 'You have to be dedicated and determined. You need to create a learning environment. And there has to be goodwill between the teachers and the students.'

Source: Dean Nelson, *Sunday Times*, 29th June 2008.

# Answers – Unit 15

**2**  Text 15A: summary of what Panupong does and why:

When he can afford it, he spends the night driving a medically equipped vehicle around the city of Bangkok in order to be able to come to the aid of victims of accidents after he receives an emergency call. He gives CPR to those whose hearts have stopped. He earns money for the cause by giving talks as a lecturer or guest speaker.

Although he receives no pay, Panupong feels responsible for the people in need of medical attention and is completely dedicated to the job, despite having been badly injured in the past when rushing to an emergency call. He is proud to be doing a useful service and says it gives value to his life. He feels sympathy for the suffering of fellow humans and believes they have the right to medical care. Sometimes he is discouraged by the thought that he alone can change nothing, but he cannot bear the thought of not being available in case someone is dying and he could save them.

**5**  Text 15B: Babur's day:
- He rises at 5 a.m. for morning prayers.
- He does household chores then takes bus to his school 5 km away.
- School starts at 10 a.m. and he works at his lessons for six hours.
- At 4 p.m. he takes off his uniform.
- He goes to teach 650 pupils in the village school.
- He has ten helpers, volunteer teachers aged 16–19.
- His second school starts at 5 p.m.
- He teaches English, Bengali, History and Maths.
- He finishes at 8 p.m.
- He is not tired at the end of the day; this is his vocation; determination keeps him energetic.

**8**  Fundraising speeches (including inferences):

Panupong needs money for: petrol for the ambulance; to be able to afford to go on patrol every night; to provide shelter for the homeless; to run basic first aid courses for the public; to increase the number of people and vehicles in the team.

Babur needs money for: more staff to make classes smaller; more books and furniture; to enable himself to become properly qualified; to extend the scheme to more Bengali villages.

# Directed writing

## Unit 16 To board or not to board

### Topic outline

- **Syllabus component:** Paper 3 question 1; Paper 1; Paper 6 task 2
- **Main skills:** directed writing; genre transformation
- **Secondary skills:** paraphrasing; selecting material; developing material; argument style
- **Outcome:** worksheet; argument dialogue; persuasive speech; persuasive letter; paired speaking; *argument dialogue; *leaflet
- **Materials:** school magazine articles; Worksheet for Text 16A: A boarder's view
- **Texts:** Text 16A: A boarder's view; Text 16B: The boarding experience

### Lesson plan

1. Ask students to read Text 16A. (5)

2. Give out Worksheet for Text 16A and ask students to complete it. (15)

3. Ask students to check their answers. Collect the completed worksheets to assess. (5)

4. Ask students to underline or highlight the words or phrases in paragraphs 1, 2 and 3 of Text 16A which best convey the feelings of the writer in a new country. (5)

5. Invite responses and collect on the board. Discuss why these words are effective. (5)

6. Ask students to prepare the answer, of about half a side, the writer might give if one of his children asked to be allowed to go abroad to boarding school. They will need to develop the ideas in Text 16A. (10)

7. Invite students to read out their answers. Judge whether they contain inference, development, persuasiveness, voice, audience. (10)

8. Ask students to read Text 16B. (5)

9. Ask students to identify features of argumentative style in Text 16B and give examples (e.g. short sentences, parallel structures, antithesis, repetition for effect, emphatic verbs, use of first person, use of absolutes). (5)

10. Ask students, in pairs, to underline or highlight in Text 16B the points in favour of boarding education. (5)

11. Ask students, in pairs, to collect ideas for questions and answers from both texts and to script an argumentative dialogue between the writers of Texts 16A and 16B, who should each speak at least five times. They should include the stylistic features identified in task 9. (10)

12. Invite pairs to perform their dialogues. Vote on the best dialogue, based on the range of material used and the persuasiveness of the speakers. (10)

### Homework task

Your friend has been offered by his/her parents the chance of going to a boarding school in another country. Plan and write a letter to your friend of one and a half sides, pointing out the things to be said for and against accepting the offer, based on the evidence in the two texts, and giving your own opinion.

### Additional tasks

a. Ask students to write a dialogue between parents who are arguing about whether to send their child to boarding school.

b. Ask students to write a promotional leaflet for their school, using some of the ideas from Text 16B and relevant ones of their own. They should write one side of paper.

# Text 16A

# A BOARDER'S VIEW

I remember vividly that cold, dark Sunday evening 50 years ago when my parents first drove me to my new school, where the head received us in his study. Having only a few weeks earlier travelled by ship from East Africa, East Yorkshire in January was a shock. After pleasantries over a cup of tea, my parents left to make the long journey back to Dar es Salaam. I shall never forget that feeling of being left utterly alone. I remember tears welling up and the head telling me that I would have to grow up. He and I were never to get on. The following term, for no reason I could ever discern, he confiscated my favourite miniature car, which I kept in my locker. I never got it back.

For a child who had spent all his previous life in tropical open spaces, the north of England was an awful place. Where I came from, the sun shone, there were palm trees, white sandy beaches, mangoes, houses with big gardens. I never saw a mango in Yorkshire; houses were joined to each other in terraces, and it was eternally dark and cold. Short trousers were a trial for an 11-year-old with hypothermia. I worked my way along corridors pressing my knees to radiators to restore circulation.

Life improved in some ways, but the long separation from the land that was home to me was something I never came to terms with. Like many others of my generation sent away to school in England, there was to be only one trip home a year, which was for the summer holiday. At Christmas and Easter I was parked with various relatives in unfamiliar towns. They took good care of me but they were strangers, albeit of a different kind. The school, with its long established traditions imbued with an ethos fresh from the nineteenth century, was a place I never came to terms with. If you were academically able or good at cricket – or better still, both – it served you well. If not, that was your problem, not the school's.

Boarding school certainly makes one self-reliant, which comes in handy later in life. After that experience I had no problem surviving military academy. It was noticeable how much better the ex-boarders tended to fare in training than those who had been at day schools. But it can impair the parental connection – I never forgave mine for sending me away. For some reason I held my father to blame, which created a rift which was never properly mended, despite his very best efforts. I understand now, of course, that from my parents' perspective it would have seemed the most sensible course of action at the time.

My own experience and that of my wife Geraldine (who was sent to a convent boarding school) turned us against boarding for our own three children (even assuming we could have afforded it). But the world has changed markedly for the better. I have no doubt that these days boarding schools are far kinder places than once they were. And by the way, if anyone finds a coin under the floor of the dormitory on the top floor, it's mine; it rolled across the floor and dropped between the floorboards in February 1958.

Adapted from 'A boarder's view' by Donald McGregor, in the 'Alternative Old Pocklington Bulletin'.

Text 16B

# THE BOARDING EXPERIENCE:

## The case for the defence by a boarding school head

Sending children away to boarding school has been a controversial idea for some years now. Many other cultures view this British habit as at best incomprehensible and at worst tantamount to child abuse – the latter image encouraged by a number of notorious fictional representations. It is true that, until the 1960s, British boarding-school education was often rather spartan in nature, and even cruel at times. This was a hangover from the perceived role of 'public schools' in preparing army officers and imperial civil servants for the hardships they would endure in their careers of public service.

All this has changed. Anybody who visits a British boarding school today comes away with an overwhelming impression of a happy, busy, motivated community of well-adjusted young people who are cared for and who live in comfortable, personalised living spaces. The era of huge, impersonal dormitories is long gone, as are inhuman matrons and housemasters. Boarding education today reflects the wider revolution which has taken place in education in the past thirty years: student-centred, skills-based learning has replaced 'chalk-and-talk' and 'rote learning'. There is a profound emphasis on developing the individual, on helping and encouraging every student to achieve their best in whichever fields they have talent.

Many parents find it an agonising decision to send their beloved children away from home for three quarters of the year. They do it not because they are indifferent to their children; on the contrary, they do it because they care deeply about them and wish to give them the best opportunities and foundations for adulthood that they can. Boarding schools understand the sacrifice which parents are making, and communicate regularly with them. Most boarding schools operate an 'open-door' policy under which parents are welcome to visit the school at any time and to attend all school events.

A substantial proportion of boarding school students live overseas, many of them in places where a decent education is simply not available. Many others live in rural areas where the daily drive to a good school would destroy the quality of life for the children.

Although there are of course good maintained schools in many parts of Britain, even the best cannot provide the range and quality of education which boarding schools can offer. In a boarding school, classes are smaller; staff are more highly qualified; there is an overriding commitment to a broad vision of education which does not end at 3 o'clock or at the classroom door. All boarding schools offer exceptional programmes of sporting, artistic, intellectual, cultural and physical activities. Any student with any special talent, interest or pursuit will find that it is nurtured by caring and patient staff at a boarding school. Because students are in the school seven days a week, so are the staff, and the students' time is employed fruitfully throughout the week.

The same is true for those who have special educational needs. The supportive atmosphere and the 24-hour-a day availability of specialist staff mean that children who need help receive far more than can be offered in a day school.

Pastoral care is at the heart of boarding school life. Every adult in the school makes it their business to get to know each student, both in the classroom and beyond, and to offer them the opportunity to share their concerns and problems and to receive appropriate advice and guidance.

A key feature of the boarding-school experience which is not always appreciated is the educational value of learning to live together in a community: to get on with other people from a range of backgrounds, to share challenges and adventures together, to learn how to overcome adversity and cope with occasional failure, and to learn how to be a member of a team. Young people also, of course, learn to be independent, confident, self-reliant: in a word, they grow up faster and more successfully than those who have been sheltered at home. They are manifestly better-equipped for the transition to university and the workplace. They understand the importance of being a member of a community, and they make friendships for life.

# Worksheet for Text 16A: A boarder's view

1. Why did the writer find East Yorkshire *a shock*? [1]

2. Explain in your own words the meaning of *pleasantries over a cup of tea*. [1]

3. Give the phrase which best describes how distressed the writer felt after his parents left him. [1]

4. Explain, using your own words, *He and I were never to get on*. [2]

5. State three ways in which the English landscape differed from that of Africa. [3]

6. What effect does the writer achieve by saying that he was *parked with various relatives*? [2]

7. Explain in your own words the two things he *never came to terms with*. [2]

8. Explain in your own words what, in the writer's view, ex-boarders have which day-school pupils lack. [2]

9. Put into your own words the phrase *impair the parental connection*. [2]

10. What two things is the writer implying by saying *even assuming we could have afforded it*? [2]

11. Give two reasons why the writer tells us that he lost a coin under the floorboards of his dormitory. [2]

[Total: 20 marks]

# Answers to Worksheet for Text 16A: A boarder's view

1  Why did the writer find East Yorkshire *a shock*? [1]

   **It was cold and dark compared to East Africa.**

2  Explain in your own words the meaning of *pleasantries over a cup of tea*. [1]

   **trivial polite conversation at tea-time**

3  Give the phrase which best describes how distressed the writer felt after his parents left him. [1]

   **'tears welling up'**

4  Explain, using your own words, *He and I were never to get on.* [2]

   **We continued to dislike each other/we did not manage to become friendly**

5  State three ways in which the English landscape differed from that of Africa. [3]

   **There was less sun, the vegetation was not tropical, and there was much less space.**

6  What effect does the writer achieve by saying that he was *parked with various relatives*? [2]

   **He conveys the impression that he was being dumped on people he didn't know well and who didn't really want him.**

7  Explain in your own words the two things he *never came to terms with*. [2]

   **He was never reconciled to being away from home, or to the the school's atmosphere being so old-fashioned.**

8  Explain in your own words what, in the writer's view, ex-boarders have which day-school pupils lack. [2]

   **the ability to be depend on themselves and the ability to cope with disciplined training**

9  Put into your own words the phrase *impair the parental connection*. [2]

   **damage the relationship with one's mother and father**

10  What two things is the writer implying by saying *even assuming we could have afforded it*? [2]

   **He is implying that boarding schools are very expensive, and that he and his wife were not well off.**

11  Give two reasons why the writer tells us that he lost a coin under the floorboards of his dormitory. [2]

   **He is pointing out that he slept in a room with bare floorboards and no carpet when he was at school, and that he has not forgotten any of the distressing experiences he had when he was there.**

[Total: 20 marks]

# Answers – Unit 16

**3** See Worksheet for Text 16A answers.

**4** Text 16A – words conveying writer's feelings:

Paragraph 1 – *shock, alone*

Paragraph 2 – *awful, dark and cold*

Paragraph 3 – *trial, separation from ... home, unfamiliar, strangers*

**6** Text 16A: writer's answer to his children:

Certainly not. My boarding school was a cold, unkind place and I was not happy there. You would feel very lonely, and there would probably be at least one teacher you didn't get on with and who was even cruel to you. The environment and climate would be very different from here and you would be homesick. It might not always be possible for you to come home for every school holiday, and you would hate being dumped on distant relatives. There are no luxuries and home comforts, you know; they don't even have carpet on the floor and you have to sleep in a dormitory with lots of other pupils and no privacy. Only students who are very academic or very sporty really enjoy boarding school. You might grow away from the family and would never forgive me for letting you go, just as I never forgave my own father. Although boarding schools are character-building – and they might have improved somewhat nowadays – I wouldn't want to take the risk of your being as unhappy as your mother and I were.

**10** Text 16B: points in favour of boarding:
- parents abroad or living in remote parts cannot find suitable local education
- children's special talents and interests are nurtured
- children with special needs can do better in boarding schools
- boarding schools have a unity of aim
- there is good communication with parents
- it is an act of love and self-sacrifice to offer your child such an opportunity
- boarders make full use of time
- there is a wide range of opportunities and new experiences on offer
- boarders learn self-reliance in a supportive environment
- boarding schools offer a totality of experience, full of challenges
- no problem or personal issue can be ignored
- they can achieve much more than day schools in terms of developing the individual
- the staff have detailed knowledge of every pupil
- they offer the enriching experience of community life
- pupils make deep and life-long friendships

# Composition – argument

## Unit 17 Fur and against

**Topic outline**

- **Syllabus component:** Paper 3 section 2 question 2; Paper 3 section 1; Paper 2 question 3; *coursework assignment 3
- **Main skills:** argumentative writing; summary
- **Secondary skills:** structuring argument; supporting views; persuasive devices; evaluating argument; adopting viewpoint; group discussion
- **Outcome:** formal letter; argument composition; *coursework type 3
- **Materials:** magazine article; campaign website; argument writing structure handout
- **Texts:** Text 17A: Fur and against; Text 17B: Fur FAQs

## Lesson plan

1. Ask students to give their opinion on the wearing of animal fur, with reasons. (10)

2. Ask students to read Text 17A. (5)

3. Ask students to re-read Text 17A, highlighting each point in the argument in favour of the wearing of fur, and to compile a list. (5)

4. Read out or write points on board and ask students to amend their list. (5)

5. Ask students, in pairs, to identify in Text 17A a) the structure of the article, and b) the devices employed to persuade the reader. (10)

6. Ask students, in pairs, to think of questions to ask representatives of the anti-fur campaign. (5)

7. Choose students to read out Text 17B. Comment on the number of questions correctly anticipated in task 6. (5)

8. Invite students to say which fact in Text 17B they found the most persuasive, and why. (5)

9. Ask students to decide, giving reasons and examples, whether Text 17A or 17B is more strongly argued and has more persuasive devices. Ask whether any of them have changed their view since the opening discussion, and if so why. (5)

10. Ask students to turn the answers in Text 17B into a letter to the editor of the *Sunday Times* from PETA in response to the article by AA Gill. (They should address and refute several of the points in Text 17A, and pay particular attention to the structuring and sequencing of their letter.) (20)

11. Ask students to swap letters, suggest improvements, and then correct their own responses. Collect them for assessment as a directed writing task. (5)

12. Ask students to plan an argumentative composition for or against the claim: 'Animals are on this planet for the benefit of humans' (see CD-ROM for argument writing structure handout). Their composition should have a logical and linked structure similar to that identified in task 5 a. (They may use ideas from Texts 17A and 17B if adapted and supported with different examples.) (10)

## Homework task

Write your argumentative composition, using between 350 and 450 words. You should check it and improve it before giving it in for assessment. (Mark out of 13 for content and structure; mark out of 12 for style and accuracy.)

## Additional tasks

a. Ask students to analyse, evaluate and give their own opinion on the views expressed in Text 17A, as a coursework assignment type 3.

b. Play an argument game in pairs. Give each pair a moral dilemma question to debate in two minutes. For example: You don't want to participate in the school swimming gala but find your name is on the list. Do you fake illness to get out of it? One student argues the case for and the other the case against, giving as many reasons as they can in the time allowed. The class vote on which student gave the most persuasive answer.

# Text 17A

# FUR
## and against

… Our most distant ancestors came through the Ice Age without going black with frostbite because they wore second-hand skin: fur. We are, as I'm sure even the least perceptive of you will have noticed, nude underneath our pyjamas. Naked apes. We don't have enough hair, fur, fluff or feathers to deflect even the finest drizzle. We shiver in pathetically bald bodies for a reason – and the reason is that we look better in suede than cows do. …

We shed our thick short and curlies because it was our natural selection, our destiny, our personal ecology, and instead gained those uniquely human attributes: taste and vanity. We wore other species' skins when they had no further use for them, and we've been doing it for a long time. How fur went from being practical and chic, stylish and sensible for 100,000 years, and then all of a sudden became the coat of shame in the past decade, is one of the oddest about-faces in all civilisation.

There have always been people who are funny about their relationship with animals – vegetarians who got religion, a few people who swept the street in front of them so as not to hurt a flightless fly – but the majority of us, the vast, vast majority, have gone on eating anything dumb enough to taste good with chips, and squashing cockroaches wherever possible. But that odd prejudice, the fatwa on fur, has become automatic and universal in our select and ethically compromised bit of the First World. The virulence and viciousness of fur vigilantes mean that few of us now brave the spittle-flecked venom of self-righteous pressure groups and dim, new-age absolutists. The argument against fur has always been more about class and money than about dumb critters. Fur, restricted to the point of prohibitive expense, is now symbolic of wealth and power.

Enough. A number of furriers are now taking back the morality of skin. They are mostly from the north – Scandinavia, Greenland, Russia and Iceland – where fur has always been a practical business in a most practical part of the world. In Denmark, fur is an agricultural business. That famously dictatorial, cruel and authoritarian society farms more mink than any other country, and it does so in conditions that most Danish pigs could only dream of. Of all the animals that we kill for our personal use, mink have by far and away the easiest passing: well fed and unstressed, they're gently gassed.

One of my favourite shops is a remarkable

furrier in Reykjavik. Eggert Johannsson makes beautiful, sensible clothes out of pelts. He is a missionary for what he calls 'ethical fur': well sourced, responsibly farmed and humanely culled. Seals, for instance. The European Union is debating whether to ban sealskin on anyone except a seal. In Greenland, hunting them is the subsistence income of the east coast. It's what they do. It's what they've always done. There is nothing else to do. There is nothing else. They can't grow cut flowers instead. In Iceland, parts of the shore where the seals congregate were sold as agricultural assets. Farmers would facilitate the natural seal colonies, protecting them from predators, and once a year they'd cull them. But since the seal market has collapsed, so have the care and value of the shoreline, and so have the seals. All over the North Sea, their populations are fluctuating. They're caught in fishing nets, shot by fishermen. They hang around ports and fish farms like water foxes. The seals have gone from being valuable, protected and plentiful, to being waterborne vermin and endangered, because we have removed their value thanks to ignorant squeamishness and class politics.

The argument goes that once we may have needed fur, but now we don't; we have, instead, technology. Well, leaving aside the aesthetics of real, I assume you all know how polymers such as nylon, polyester, Terylene and so on are made. That they use fossil fuels, and intensely polluting processes that involve some of the most toxic chemicals on the planet. ... I've been there. I've seen the greatest environmental disaster on the globe, greater than an armful of runways or nuclear bombs, worse than deforestation or any city's urban sprawl: the murder of the Aral Sea in central Asia by the drying-up of the Oxus River, reducing an area the size of Denmark to a toxic, salted dust bowl – and all caused by cotton. [...] Compared with a cotton shirt, a fur coat is morally blameless.

The most poignant argument for fur is not where it comes from, or who first wore it; it's what it looks like and how it feels. A polyamide coat connects you to an oil well and a factory; fur joins you to your heritage. It is 100,000 years of history and culture. We wear fur because it is our story. If you haven't put on a fur coat recently, or ever, try it. Cast aside your prejudice and feel it. You can sense it's not simply a statement of fashion, wealth or even warmth; the connection is ancient, truly visceral. Fur is the cover, the binding, of our long, long, story. And if you're still not convinced, then would you for a moment consider your own cushions, your pillow. The feathers inside, the bird fur, where do you imagine that came from? How do you imagine all that duck and goose skin was gleaned? I'd hate for you to be a hypocrite. Sleep well.

Source: AA Gill, *Sunday Times*, 7th December 2008.

# Text 17B

# Fur FAQs (PETA)*

*Aren't there laws to protect animals on fur farms?*

Currently, there are no federal laws providing protection for the millions of animals – including chinchillas, foxes, minks, and raccoons – who suffer and die on fur farms. The fur industry remains completely self-regulated, which means that animals are kept in crowded, filthy wire cages, where they often develop neurotic behaviors and become sick or wounded, and fur farmers kill them by breaking their necks while they are fully conscious or by electrocuting them. Click here to see pictures of caged animals on fur farms.

**Isn't animal fur more environmentally friendly than synthetic fur?**

Absolutely not! Fur has fallen so far from grace that furriers are now trying to convince consumers that pelts are 'eco-friendly', but furs are loaded with chemicals to keep them from decomposing in buyers' closets, and fur production pollutes the environment and wastes precious resources. It takes more than 15 times as much energy to produce a fur coat from ranch-raised animals than it does to produce a fake fur. Plus, the waste produced on fur farms poisons our waterways. And don't forget … unlike faux fur, the 'real thing' causes millions of animals to suffer every year. Click here for more information about fur and the environment.

**Animals in cages on fur farms don't suffer that much because they've never known anything else, right?**

Wrong! Animals on fur farms are prevented from acting on their most basic instinctual behaviors, which causes them tremendous suffering. Even animals who have been caged since birth feel the need to move around, groom themselves, stretch their limbs, and exercise. All confined animals suffer from intense boredom – some so severely that they begin displaying neurotic behaviors such as pacing, turning in endless circles, self-mutilation, and even cannibalism. Click here to learn more about cruelty on fur farms.

**Aren't animals better off on fur farms, where they are fed and protected, than they are out in the wild, where they can die of starvation, disease, or predation?**

A similar argument was used to support the claim that black people were better off being slaves on plantations than being free men and women! Animals on fur farms suffer so much that it is inconceivable that they could be worse off in the wild. The wild isn't 'wild' to the animals who live there – it's their home. The fact that they might suffer there is no reason to ensure that they suffer in captivity. Click here to learn more about what a lifetime in a cage is like.

### Is the fur industry as cruel as people make it out to be?

It's even crueller. PETA's undercover investigations on fur farms have found that animals are killed by anal electrocution, during which an electrically charged steel rod is inserted into the animal's rectum, literally frying his or her insides. Exposed broken bones, upper respiratory infections, and cancerous tumors were among the wounds and diseases that animals endured without veterinary treatment on one fur farm that we investigated.

Animals caught in steel-jaw leghold traps are in so much pain that some actually chew off their limbs in order to escape. Since they are unable to eat, keep warm, or defend themselves against predators, many die in horrible ways before the trapper arrives to kill them. Others suffer in the traps for days until they are caught and killed. To avoid damaging the pelt, trappers often beat or stomp animals to death. Whether they are enduring the excruciating pain of a leghold trap or a lifetime of agony in a tiny cage, these animals suffer immensely. Click here to learn more about fur trapping.

### Is it true that some companies actually use dog and cat fur in their products?

Unfortunately, yes. There is a thriving dog- and cat-fur industry in Asia. Most of this fur is falsely labeled as 'rabbit fur' or simply not labeled at all. Dog and cat skin is made into fur coats, fur figurines, and leather shoes, which are sold to unsuspecting consumers in America. Without expensive DNA tests, it is virtually impossible to know exactly what kind of animal you are wearing if you choose to buy fur. And if you wouldn't wear your dog, why wear the fur of any animal? Click here to learn more about the dog- and cat-fur industry.

### Why should animals have rights?

Supporters of animal rights believe that animals have an inherent worth – a value completely separate from their usefulness to humans. We believe that every creature with a will to live has a right to live free from pain and suffering. For more information, click here.

Adapted from: www.furisdead.com

*PETA – People for the Ethical Treatment of Animals

# Answers – Unit 17

**3**  Text 17A: summary points pro fur: [14 points]
- long tradition of wearing fur
- humans don't have enough natural hair/are meant to use animal skins
- it's only a recent and passing fad to feel ashamed of wearing fur
- the majority of humans are meat-eaters
- we kill insects
- pressure groups have made people afraid to wear it
- anti-fur campaigners don't care about animals, only about the politics of class/wealth
- modern fur farms kill animals humanely
- some countries' economies are dependent on the sale of animal skins
- animals have a more painful death if not culled by furriers
- some species have become endangered by the collapse of the fur market
- the production of fake fur and even natural materials involves the use of pollutants and toxic chemicals
- the look and feel of fur is wonderful, and part of our natural heritage
- we use feathers, a type of animal fur, in bedding so it's hypocritical to be against fur coats

**5**  **a**  Text 17A: argument stages:

1  gives historical and scientific facts

2  cites normal human behaviour

3  attacks motives of the extremists

4  informs us of humane approaches of furriers of northern 'practical' nations

5  points out inconsistency that animals killed for fur suffer less pain than those killed for meat, so if we allow one, why not the other?

6  introduces personal acquaintance as evidence

7  uses positive-sounding terminology of 'ethical fur'

8  pleads on behalf of countries which have no other industry

9  claims that seals are now suffering because of ignorant and politically motivated anti-fur activists

10  dismisses ecological argument against fur production by claiming other fabrics cause more pollution

11  returns to the beginning, the heritage argument that it is natural and right for humans to wear fur and only the prejudiced won't admit how good it looks and feels

12  says anyone who owns a feather-stuffed cushion is a hypocrite if they are against fur coats

**b**  Text 17A: persuasive devices:

humorous comparisons; irony (*flightless fly*); mockery; insult (*spittle-flecked*); ridicule; short and non sentences (*Seals, for instance.*); surprise information (about cotton); reversing common beliefs; derogatory description of animals as *dumb critters*; use of triple structures (*well sourced, responsibly farmed and humanely culled*); use of abrupt command (*Enough, try it*); accusing the reader of prejudice and hypocrisy; analogy and antithesis; rhetorical questions; alliteration (*virulence and viciousness of fur vigilantes*); personal testimony (*I've been there*); switch from inclusive *we* to accusatory *you* in final paragraph; conclusive, dismissive and sarcastic final sentence.

**9** Which text is more persuasive and why:

Text 17A is more personal in its attack on the hypocrisy of the reader. It uses wit to woo the reader, and mockery to make the reader not want to be associated with 'self-righteous' pressure groups, who are blamed for making it possible for only the rich to be able to afford the fur which should be available for everyone, and so raises anger against them. It has a large number of points to make to support its case.

Text 17B uses shocking factual material and attacks what it sees as the myths which the pro-fur lobby uses to defend its position. The 'click here' commands imply that a wealth of evidence, including photographic proof, exists to support their case, which has been based on extensive research. The emphasis throughout is on the pain and suffering of animals trapped and killed for their coats, and this evokes pity in the reader.

Either text can be chosen as the answer to this question: both texts have widened the issue from fur coats to the environment and pollution in order to influence a wider group than just animal lovers. However, the most persuasive device of all is a linked and progressive structure to the stages of an argument, so Text 17A is perhaps more effective overall, although Text B has the greater emotional impact.

# Composition – argument

## Unit 18 Google generation

**Topic outline**

- **Syllabus component:** Paper 3 section 2 question 2; Paper 2 question 3; Paper 3 section 1; Paper 6 task 3; coursework assignment 1
- **Main skills:** argumentative writing; discursive writing
- **Secondary skills:** summarising; identifying material; collating material; rhetorical devices; group discussion
- **Outcome:** argument composition; summary; *Paper 6 task 3; *coursework task 1
- **Materials:** newspaper articles; rhetorical devices handout; argument writing structure handout
- **Texts:** Text 18A: The beep and the ping; Text 18B: TXTNG: the gr8 db8; Text 18C: Digital divide; Text 18D: Discomgoogolating; Text 18E: Email monster

## Lesson plan

1. Tell students the original title and new title of Text 18A: 'Stoopid' and 'The beep and the ping'. Ask them to guess what the argument will be about. (5)

2. Ask students to read Text 18A. (5)

3. Give students the handout on rhetorical devices (see page 108 or CD-ROM) and ask them, in pairs, to find and highlight as many as possible in Text 18A. (5)

4. Collect feedback and discuss the effect of the devices in Text 18A (the overall effect is polemical). (5)

5. Ask students, in pairs, to re-read Text 18A and to collect arguments for the claim that the Internet is destroying human intelligence. (5)

6. Collect feedback in students' own words and record on the board as an 'Against' list. (5)

7. Ask students to skim Text 18B for gist and say in one sentence what it is about. (5)

8. Ask students, in pairs, to reduce Text 18B to bullet points (i.e. remove examples, direct speech, repetition, imagery, minor details). (10)

9. Elicit and add the agreed points to the board as a 'For' list. (5)

10. Ask students to read Text 18C. (5)

11. Put students into groups of four and ask them to discuss the arguments in Texts 18A, 18B (see lists on board) and 18C on whether technology is damaging or enabling. Ask them to take notes on the views expressed and the examples given. Go around the class, assessing the quality of the discussion (which could be for a paper 6 group activity assessment). (15)

12. Ask students to read Text 18D and to summarise it in no more than 100 words, without losing any of the information. (10)

13. Invite students to read out their summaries and comment as a class on appropriateness of content and concision of style. (5)

14. Ask students to read Text 18E, noting how the style is different from that of Texts 18A and 18B (i.e. because this is discursive/informative and not argumentative writing). (5)

## Homework task

Using all five texts, notes taken during the lesson, and other ideas of your own, plan an argument composition entitled: 'Does technology make us more knowledgeable and efficient or just more stressed?' They should use the argument writing structure (see CD-ROM) and include persuasive devices from the task 3 handout.

## Additional task

Invite students in turn to give an impromptu talk to the class for three minutes on a current news topic. The topics can be the kind of issue which generates discussion on blogs and Twitter sites (e.g. recent political events, legal battles, natural disasters, announcements by celebrities).

© Cambridge University Press 2010

# Text 18A

# The beep and the ping

On Wednesday I received 72 emails, not counting junk. It was therefore a quiet day in man's harassment by self-inflicted technology. The opposite of attention is distraction, an unnatural condition and one which kills. Chronic distraction is as dangerous as cigarette smoking. There is the great myth of multi-tasking, but no human being can effectively write an email and speak on the telephone. Both activities use language and the language channel in the brain can't cope. Multi-taskers fool themselves by rapidly switching attention and, as a result, their output deteriorates. There is evidence that people in distracted jobs are, in early middle age, appearing with the same symptoms of burn-out as air traffic controllers. They might have stress-related diseases, even irreversible brain damage, but this is not caused by overwork but by multiple distracted work.

Mark Bauerlein, professor of English at Emory University in Atlanta, has just written *The Dumbest Generation: How the digital age stupefies young Americans and jeopardises our future.* He portrays a bibliophobic generation of teens, incapable of sustaining concentration long enough to read a book. In an influential essay in The Atlantic magazine, Nicholas Carr asks: 'Is Google making us stupid?' Carr, a chronic distractee like the rest of us, noticed that he was finding it increasingly difficult to immerse himself in a book or long article. Instead he now Googles his way through life, scanning and skimming, not pausing to think, to absorb. He says 'We now go outside of ourselves to make all the connections that we used to make inside of ourselves.' The next generation, loving novelty but craving depth, will not realise what they have lost.

People make big money out of distracting us, so what can be done? Tests clearly show that a switched-on television reduces the quality and quantity of interaction between children and their parents. The Internet multiplies the effect a thousandfold. Paradoxically, the supreme information provider also has the effect of reducing information intake. Teenagers go to their laptops on coming home from school and sink into their online cocoon; but 90% of sites visited by teenagers are social networks. They are immersed not in knowledge but in gossip and banter. All Internet connections are threadbare; they lack the complexity and depth of real-world interactions. So called Facebook 'friends' are just casual, tenuous electronic pings. Nothing could be further removed from the idea of friendship, in which people stick together through thick and thin.

Kids are just skimming the surface of life, and we are all becoming infantilised cyber-serfs, as well as cyber-surfers, our entertainments and impulses maintained and controlled by the techno-geek aristocracy. The computer is training us not for survival, but to drown in the sea of information. People need to be retrained to pay attention, to concentrate, to focus. They need to be taught how to turn off and to ignore the beep and the ping.

Adapted from 'Stoopid: why the Google generation isn't as smart as it thinks' by Bryan Appleyard, *Sunday Times*, 20th July 2008.

# TXTNG: the gr8 db8

Language changes and evolves constantly. Some people get very worked up about this; most quietly use new coinings because, very often, they are useful. But the arrival of text-messaging on mobile phones seems to have introduced a new threat to the language which many people seem to believe will be fatal. An extraordinary amount of rage has been generated – at least in the kind of newspapers read by older and more conservative readers – by the use of simple abbreviations to save time (and money) in text messages.

Now David Crystal, our most respected commentator on contemporary language and its uses and abuses, has entered this contentious arena. He is also honorary professor of linguistics at the University of Wales, so if anyone knows what he is talking about in the 'Great Debate' about 'texting' (or 'txtng') it should be him. And his position, as stated very clearly in this persuasive book, is that the whole issue has been hyped absurdly - largely by those too old to use texting at all.

Crystal's opponents have made some extravagant claims about the damage that texting can do: 'Texting is bleak, bald, sad shorthand which masks dyslexia, poor spelling and mental laziness', one commentator claimed. Another said 'Texters are vandals doing to our language what Genghis Khan did to his neighbours 800 years ago'.

All this is to be seen, of course, in the context of an anguished national debate about declining standards of literacy among young people, and the alleged replacement of reading in a whole generation by addiction to computer and mobile phone screens. But old people have always decried the new crazes of the young, generally without understanding them.

Crystal's view is, first of all, that we have been here before, many times over the past century, and that the English language has proved remarkably resilient. Secondly, he argues that texting actually helps children's literacy, because for many it is a new functional form of communication which is written and not verbal. So what if they introduce some abbreviations? Crystal writes, 'I do not see how texting could be a significant factor when discussing children who have real problems with literacy. It you have difficulty with reading and writing you are hardly going to be predisposed to use a technology which demands sophisticated abilities in reading and writing.'

The truth is, he claims, that older adults feel excluded because they do not know what 'LOL' stands for when their grandchild uses it to end a text (does it mean 'Lots Of Love', or 'Laugh Out Loud'? It all depends on the context). But would they rather receive no communication at all?

In any case, Crystal points out that many of the popular beliefs about texting may be unfounded. Some of the abbreviations have been in existence since long before mobile phones were invented, and are extensively used in e-mails. Some of the more extreme examples appear in texting 'dictionaries' but are rarely, if ever, actually used. More than half of all text messages consist of one sentence at most. There are, he concludes, more worthy targets for people to turn their indignation against.

# Text 18C

## DIGITAL DIVIDE

- More than 1.5 billion people worldwide have some sort of access to the Internet.
- 5 billion people, 75% of the world's population, do not.
- Most of these people live outside the developed Western countries.
- 74% of North America is online, just over half of European households, 28% of the Middle East, but only 6.9% of the population of Africa.
- Cost of computers and network connectivity has come down in the West and in the developing nations.
- There has been a global rise in the number of Internet cafes opened even in small towns.
- There is an unexamined assumption that the Internet is on its way to being generally available to all who want it.
- The gap in the access to and use of the latest information and communications technology – computers, mobile phones, digital networks, interactive television – is as wide as ever.
- The consequences of the divide are being felt in the poorer parts of the world.
- As much as access to clean water, health care, food quantity and quality, and educational opportunity, access to technology has an impact of all aspects of life.
- The web and email are gateways to other resources – cheaper ones than text books – and to domestic self-reliance and to professional development.
- Being able to answer one's questions for oneself is one of the most enabling tools there is, and the basis for lifelong self-supported learning.
- Few politicians now talk about this digital divide as a major development issue, and there is a growing sense that it is yesterday's problem.

# Text 18D

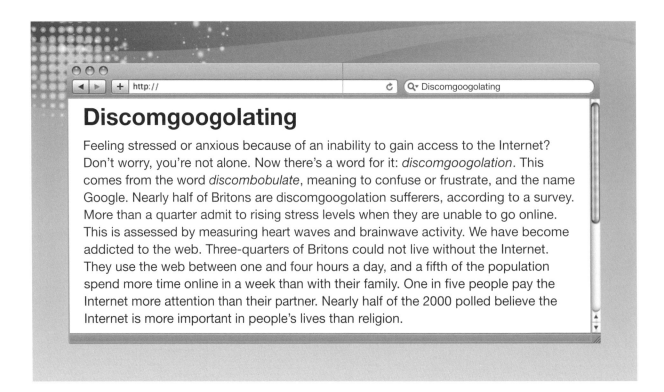

## Discomgoogolating

Feeling stressed or anxious because of an inability to gain access to the Internet? Don't worry, you're not alone. Now there's a word for it: *discomgoogolation*. This comes from the word *discombobulate*, meaning to confuse or frustrate, and the name Google. Nearly half of Britons are discomgoogolation sufferers, according to a survey. More than a quarter admit to rising stress levels when they are unable to go online. This is assessed by measuring heart waves and brainwave activity. We have become addicted to the web. Three-quarters of Britons could not live without the Internet. They use the web between one and four hours a day, and a fifth of the population spend more time online in a week than with their family. One in five people pay the Internet more attention than their partner. Nearly half of the 2000 polled believe the Internet is more important in people's lives than religion.

# Email monster

When her computer pinged the arrival of her 30,000th unanswered email, Vanessa Fox dared to fulfil the office worker's darkest fantasy: she declared 'email bankruptcy' and deleted them all.

Fox, an Internet strategist for an online property company, said she felt both 'terror and relief' as her inbox registered zero for the first time in a decade – then horror as it started filling up again at a rate of 1000 emails a day. Email overload is a problem she cannot easily solve. 'Anyone working in an office knows the feeling of guilt about not answering all the serious emails,' said Fox, 35. 'My reaction was pretty extreme, but at least it bought me some time to figure out what to do next. Email was a fantastic invention but now, even without spam, it's a nightmare to deal with.'

Fox is not alone in damning the email flood. The Friday before last, 150 engineers at the chipmaker Intel turned off their email systems for 24 hours, opting to talk to people by telephone instead. Intel said the company would run 'zero email Fridays' for the next month, then decide whether the initiative improved the flow of ideas and made people happier. One Intel engineer said it was scary. 'People were sneaking looks as their BlackBerries,' he said. 'But after a few hours just talking to people face to face or on the phone, you realise it's like being addicted to junk food – you can live without it'. Other large American firms have also asked employees to 'talk, not type' for one day a week. But the tension proved too much at one high-tech firm, where several workers said they could not stop pressing the send button!

The number of emails zapping around the world has multiplied five-fold since 2000. It is estimated that each day computers send out 40 billion personal emails, 17 billion automated alerts and 40 billion spam messages. The average American office worker receives about 140 emails a day, but rarely manages to read half of them or respond to more than a quarter. Universities have reported that students are getting panic attacks from trying to keep up with the volume of emails.

Ploys to deal with the blight of email include setting aside a certain time of day to deal with them and responding only to the most urgent. But maybe the only way to really escape is to get rich enough for someone else to read your emails for you!

Adapted from: John Harlow, *Sunday Times*, 14th October 2007.

# Rhetorical devices

*The fact is, as we said at the beginning of our discussion, that the aspiring speaker needs no knowledge of the truth about what is right or good ... In courts of justice no attention is paid whatever to the truth about such topics; all that matters is plausibility ... There are even some occasions when both prosecution and defence should positively suppress the facts in favor of probability, if the facts are improbable. Never mind the truth – pursue probability through thick and thin in every kind of speech; the whole secret of the art of speaking lies in consistent adherence to this principle.* **Socrates**

A rhetorical device is a technique of using language in a way that increases the persuasiveness of a piece of text by evoking an emotional or intellectual response in the reader or audience.

The devices below are often found in argumentative writing. The reader should be aware when such devices are being employed, as they manipulate the reader into agreeing with the writer or speaker and distract attention from the quality of the actual arguments being used.

**addressing reader as 'you'** – for intimacy and presupposition that the reader will agree

**antithesis** – to make it seem a simple two-sided issue

**aposiopesis (…)** – to make the reader imagine the rest, that which has not been said

**colloquialisms** – to create conversational effect to invite reader trust

**exclamations** – to create the impression that the writer feels passionate or shocked about the isssue

**hyperbole** – to increase the apparent power of the argument or evidence

**imperatives** – to sound authoritative and superior

**insulting vocabulary** – to ridicule opponents

**irony** – to create humour and appreciation

**juxtaposition** – to make a stark contrast which forces a comparison to be made

**lists** – to give the impression that a lot of data exists to support the writer's view

**modern idiom and trendy phrases** – to show the writer is up to date

**non-sentences** – to make the content stand out and sound decisive

**repetition** – for emphasis and memorability

**rhetorical questions** – to engage and involve the reader

**sarcasm** – for mockery of opponents so that the reader will not wish to identify with them

**short categorical sentences** – to give the impression that there can be no argument

**triple structures** – to make the statement memorable and effective

# Answers – Unit 18

4   Text 18A: rhetorical devices:

starting with a surprising statistic; contradicting the opening impression by saying that was just a *quiet day*; using strong, shocking language and claims that cannot be ignored (that distraction kills, and is as bad as smoking; *irreversible brain damage*) expressed as categorical statements not suggestions; use of absolutes (*All Internet connections are threadbare*; *no human can*; *Nothing could be further removed*); use of quotation; rhetorical questions (*so what can be done?*); reference to research (*Tests show*; *90% of sites*); antithesis for stark contrast (*loving novelty but craving depth*; *information provider ... reducing information*; *immersed not in knowledge but in gossip*; *not for survival, but to drown*); inclusive use of *we* (*we are all becoming infantilised*); memorable word play (*cyber-surfs*); threat (*controlled by the techno-geek aristocracy*; *drown in the sea of information*); triple structures for insistence (*to pay attention, to concentrate, to focus*)

5   Text 18A: arguments against e-communications:
- we are distracted by email
- distraction is dangerous and can kill
- no one is capable of multitasking effectively
- distracted work not overwork causes stress and burn out
- young people don't have the concentration to read a book
- we no longer think or absorb, only look superficially at information
- the next generation will not realise they have become de-skilled
- business has a vested interest in distracting us
- families are failing to communicate
- teenagers prefer social networks and gossip to studying and acquiring knowledge
- real friendship has been eroded
- our lives are controlled by technology

7   Text 18B: one-sentence summary:

The writer maintains that all the popular beliefs about texting are false as it does no harm at all to the English language.

8   Text 18B arguments for e-communications:
- only old people are against it, and they are against every new fashion
- honorary professor of linguistics is in favour of it
- the abbreviations are nothing new
- most of the abbreviations aren't actually used
- texting actually develops literacy skills
- doesn't affect those who have literacy problems

12  Text 18D: summary:

Discomgoogolation (a word created from a mixture of *discombobulate* and *Google*) means the anxious feeling half of the British population gets when unable to access the Internet, according to a survey which included a measurement of heart and brain activity. Three-quarters of Britons are addicted to the web – which they use up to four hours a day – leading 20% of them to spend more time with their computer than with their families and their partners; nearly half of the 2000 people polled admitted that they consider the Internet to be more important in modern life than religion.

**14** Text 18E: journalistic structure and style:

Journalism pieces are structured in such a way that they can be cut from the bottom upwards without losing essential information, which is always at the beginning. They usually start with the dramatic and attention-grabbing event or information, and end with a prediction.

Surnames are used for formality and objectivity, and to save space; ages are given as numerals after the name of the people referred to. There will usually be use of direct speech or quotation to give variety of voice and register, immediacy of impact and authority of sources. Puns, alliteration and exclamations may be used if the topic is not serious and a light-hearted tone is appropriate.

# Composition – description

## Unit 19 Prized possession

### Topic outline

- **Syllabus component:** Paper 3 section 2 question 3; Paper 5; coursework assignment 2
- **Main skills:** descriptive writing
- **Secondary skills:** figurative language
- **Outcome:** descriptive composition; *coursework type 2; *Paper 5 individual talk
- **Materials:** video; Worksheet for Unit 19: Memory box; generic mark schemes from CIE Teacher Support website
- **Texts:** Text 19: Memory box (video clip)

### Lesson plan

1. Ask students to listen to Text 19 (someone describing their most prized possession) played through a computer twice, noting length and structure as well as content (with or without digital projector): (5)

   http://teachertube.com/viewVideo.php?video_id=3987&title=Most_Prized_Possession

2. Ask students what they would keep in their own memory box, and to make a list (of no more than five items), with a reason to explain each choice. (5)

3. Invite students to tell the rest of the class about their memory boxes, using a similar length and structure to that of the video clip. (10)

4. Show students an object which has an interesting colour, shape or texture (e.g. a plant, fruit, fabric). Ask students to brainstorm as many things to say about it as possible, referring to all five senses. (10)

5. Ask students to add adjectives and imagery (similes), and words with sound effects (e.g. alliterative phrases, onomatopoeia) to their response to the 'still-life' object. The descriptive language should be not clichéd, not repeated, polysyllabic, unusual, precise (e.g. colours should be specific – not just *green* but *metallic green*, *faded green*, *olive green*). (10)

6. Invite students to offer their best descriptive phrases. Discuss what makes them effective. (5)

7. Give out Worksheet 19 and ask students to complete it. (25)

8. Ask students, in pairs, to study the generic mark schemes for descriptive compositions (print these from the CIE Teacher Support website) and underline key phrases in the grid boxes for content and style. Alternatively, use the Exam tips for Paper 3 section 2 and the descriptive writing structure handout from the CD. (5)

9. Invite feedback and collect key phrases on board. (5)

10. Ask students to make a checklist of success criteria for descriptive writing, based on the phrases on the board. (5)

11. Ask students to check their completed worksheet against the checklist to make sure they have fulfilled all the criteria, then add or remove material accordingly if necessary. (5)

### Homework task

Use your worksheet plan as the basis for the content and structure of a descriptive composition/coursework piece entitled 'My most prized possession'. Add extra material and detail, and links between paragraphs, to make it at least either 350 (composition) or 500 (coursework) words. Think about ways to improve expression and accuracy, as well as content. You may include references to narrative incidents, including dialogue, and reflective and discursive passages, provided that the main aim is descriptive and the writing is focused on your chosen possession.

### Additional task

Ask students to use their descriptive pieces to give an individual talk to the class (perhaps with their possession, or a photograph of it, as a visual aid). (This may be assessed for Speaking and Listening Paper 5 if delivered to you in private and followed by a short discussion – see CIE website for mark scheme.)

# Worksheet for Unit 19: Memory box

1. List your five most prized possessions. These may be things you are very proud of or feel sentimental about, or enjoy using or looking at.

2. Rank order them 1 to 5, putting a number next to each. Your number 1 should be the possession you would rescue first if your house were on fire.

3. Draw a rough sketch of your number 1 possession.

4. Write notes to describe your chosen possession, giving precise details of the object's size, shape, colour, texture and function. Include as many senses as possible, and create original similes.

**5** Explain how you came to possess your prized object: Who gave it to you and why? On what occasion? Where was it acquired? How long ago?

**6** Write notes on what the object makes you think about and feel, what you associate it with, and what memories are evoked by it.

**7** Write a paragraph arguing for the necessity or importance in your life of this possession, and why it would be more worth rescuing than anything else that you own.

**8** Decide on the order in which you will use the material above to form a composition, and number it accordingly.

# Answers – Unit 19

**10** Success criteria for descriptive writing:

    **a** Does the piece contain figurative language?

    **b** Is there at least one, and preferably more, adjective before each noun?

    **c** Are all five senses included, or at least implied, not just vision?

    **d** Are colour descriptions in precise shades, perhaps using compound adjectives?

    **e** Are the sentence lengths varied, with some complex sentences included?

    **f** Are there personal and imaginative elements, not just facts and statistics?

    **g** Is there some kind of logical framework giving the description form, dimension and progression?

    **h** Does the description contain vocabulary which is unusual, polysyllabic, interesting, ambitious?

    **i** Is the description free from repetition of ideas or vocabulary?

    **j** Is the description free from clichés (overused and predictable expressions)?

    **k** Is the description free from everyday verbs like *have* and *got*, and vague and immature adjectives like *nice, good, big, small*?

    **l** Do the sentences begin in different ways (avoiding beginning them all with *It*)?

    **m** Is an atmosphere evoked which engages the reader?

    **n** Is there a range of details which clearly define the ideas and images?

    **o** Does the piece have scope and variety?

    **p** Are the ideas developed and clearly sequenced?

    **q** Does the piece avoid becoming narrative-based?

# Composition – description

## Unit 20 Building dreams

**Topic outline**

- **Syllabus component:** Paper 3 section 2 question 3; Paper 4 assignment 2
- **Main skills:** descriptive writing; imagining
- **Secondary skills:** imagery building; structuring description
- **Outcome:** descriptive composition/descriptive coursework; *description of visual effects
- **Materials:** pictures of rooms; slideshows of houses; descriptive writing structure handout
- **Texts:** Picture 20A: Bollywood tent; Picture 20B: Greek village kitchen; Slideshow 20C: Dream houses (see CD-ROM)

## Lesson plan

1. Ask students to imagine a perfect bedroom, then to construct a spider diagram of descriptive phrases covering the five senses. Go around the class, prompting ideas. (10)

2. Ask students to give connotations when they hear the following materials: *wood, glass, metal, velvet, marble, leather,* and to add furnishing ideas to their bedroom diagram. (5)

3. Ask students to add colours to the diagram, and then modify them more precisely e.g. *rose pink, lemon yellow, matt black*. (5)

4. Ask students, in pairs, to rank order these size adjectives from small to large: *minuscule, gargantuan, microscopic, gigantic, minute, life-size, vast, tiny, huge, petite*. (5)

5. Ask them to write and read out a sentence describing the room they are currently in, creating interest by avoiding monosyllabic words and simple facts, and using imagery to convey precise sizes, shapes, colours, and textures. (5)

6. Put students in pairs and give one student in each pair Picture 20A. Ask them to describe it in as much detail as possible to their partner, who draws what is being described. Swap roles with Picture 20B. (10)

7. Hold up some of the drawings and comment on how they compare to the originals (these can be projected from the CD-ROM). (5)

8. Ask students to draw a plan of their ideal room, showing all the furniture and fittings. (5)

9. Ask students to label all the contents with interesting descriptions, using multiple evocative adjectives (a thesaurus may be useful). (5)

10. Ask students to extend their idea beyond their room to a vision of the kind of house the room is in, and to make notes on it. (5)

11. Play the slideshow of different types of concept houses. Describe each and judge its attractiveness. (10)

12. Ask students to add more details to their notes on their dream houses from task 10, then to draw the exterior of their ideal house. (10)

13. Give students the descriptive writing structure handout (see CD-ROM) and ask them to plan a description of the exterior and interior of their dream house, using all the notes and drawings. (10)

### Homework task

Using the descriptive writing structure handout, plan and write a description of the appearance of your dream house or your perfect room, using the notes and drawings collected in the lesson. (For exam practice, 350–400 words; as a coursework draft, 500–800 words.)

### Additional task

Find pictures by the surrealist painter René Magritte or M.C. Escher on the Internet and ask students to choose two to write about, describing the images in detail and explaining how they create their startling effects.

# Picture 20A

Bollywood tent

# Picture 20B

Greek village kitchen

116  Unit 20 ○ Building dreams

# Slideshow 20C Dream houses

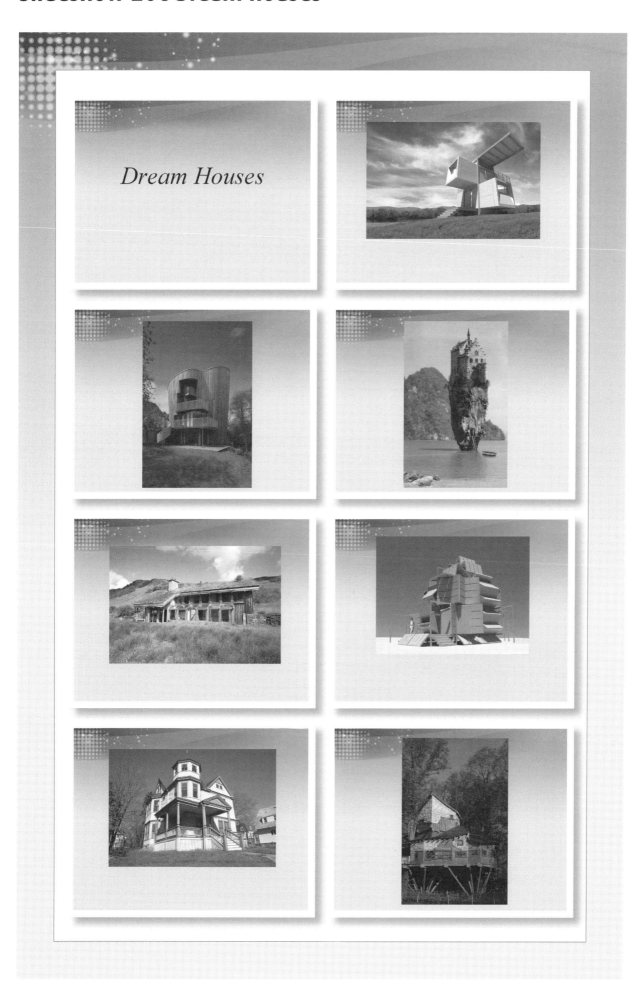

Unit 20 Building dreams

118 Unit **20 ○ Building dreams** © Cambridge University Press 2010

# Answers – Unit 20

**2** Connotations of materials:

Because materials have textures, as well as connotations of cost, historical period and geographical origin, what things are actually made of is an important factor in descriptive writing. If one is asked to imagine a teapot made of fur or chocolate, for instance, a physical reaction can be induced, so strong is our expectation that certain things can only be made of certain substances and not others. (The surrealist painters relied on the power of the associations of substances and shapes with particular objects and functions in order to shock the viewer by subverting those expectations, see Magritte in additional task.)

**3** Modifying colours:

Adding another colour to make a compound adjective, or simply saying whether it is light or dark, makes a colour reference more precise and therefore more visible to the reader. By including a reference to something else, such as a flower or a fruit, other senses are introduced (e.g. 'rose' evokes smell and texture, and 'lemon' conjures smell and taste), which intensifies the effect of the description.

**4** Rank ordering size adjectives:

There is no right answer, expect that obviously the small ones go to the left of *life-size* and the large ones go to the right. The point of the exercise is to make students aware that there are many choices of vocabulary to denote size and that there is therefore no excuse for using *big*, *little*, *small* and *large* in descriptive writing, which are dull words and convey only the vaguest impression to the reader.

# Composition – narrative

## Unit 21 Crucial decisions

**Topic outline**

- **Syllabus component:** Paper 3 Section 2 question 4; *Paper 4 assignment 2
- **Main skills:** narrative writing
- **Secondary skills:** narrative planning; *narrative openings
- **Outcome:** narrative composition/coursework type 2
- **Materials:** accounts of mountaineering accident; aspects of narrative handout
- **Text:** Text 21: The final choice

## Lesson plan

1. Ask students to consider stories they have recently read and say what needs to be considered before embarking on the writing of a story? (5)

2. Give out and discuss the handout (see pages 123–4 or CD-ROM) outlining the aspects of narrative to be decided at the planning stage. (10)

3. Ask students to read Text 21 around the class, a paragraph or few sentences each. (5)

4. Ask class to vote on which viewpoint is more exciting and why. Ask how it would have been different as a third-person narrative by someone who was in the climbing party and a witness to the event (i.e. less gripping and immediate, but first-person narrators must have survived, so this reduces tension). (5)

5. Ask students, in pairs, to identify and list the ways in which the accounts have been made engaging for the reader in terms of a) content and b) style. (10)

6. Collect feedback in two columns on board. (5)

7. Ask students to decide how they think Text 21 could end and to write a final paragraph or two as a third-person narrative, relating what happened in the morning and reconciling both viewpoints. (10)

8. Invite students to read out their endings and comment on their credibility and predictability. (5)

9. Ask students to think of a different situation and to plan a narrative with the title of 'A matter of life and death'; they should refer to the handout and the lists on the board, and include in their planning how the crisis will be resolved. (15)

10. Ask students to choose from the narrative opening options (see section **g** in the handout) and to write the opening paragraphs (about half a side) for their narrative. Whichever option they choose should set the scene and context for the main event to follow. (10)

11. Invite students to read out their openings. Vote on how effective they are in enticing the reader to read on. (10)

## Homework task

Write the narrative composition you have planned and started. It should be either 350–450 words or 500–800 words, depending on whether it is a practice composition or a coursework assignment.

## Additional task

Ask students to practise the other types of opening, for the same story, and to judge which one works best and what difference it makes to the level of reader engagement.

# Text 21

# The final choice

*As experienced mountaineers, Joe and Simon attempt the West Face of the Siula Grande in the Peruvian Andes. The ascent goes according to plan, but on the descent Joe falls and breaks his leg. His friend is lowering him down from ledge to ledge when disaster strikes.*

## Joe's account

The sense of weight on my harness increased, as did the speed. I tried braking with my arms but to no effect. I twisted round and looked up into the darkness. Rushes of snow flickered in my torch beam. I yelled for Simon to slow down. The speed increased and my heart jumped wildly. Had he lost control? I stifled the rising panic and tried to think clearly. No, he hadn't lost control, because although I was going down fast, it was steady. But there was still something wrong.

It was the slope. It was now much steeper, and that could mean only one thing – I was approaching another drop. I screamed out a frantic warning but he couldn't hear me. I shouted again, as loud as I could, but the words were whipped away into the snow clouds, and he couldn't have heard me even five metres away. I had no idea how far I was from the half-way knot. Each lowering became timeless. I slid for ever through the boiling snow without any sense of time passing – just a barely endurable period of agony.

A sense of great danger washed over me. I *had* to stop. I had to stop myself. If Simon felt my weight come off the rope he would know there must be a good reason. I grabbed my ice axe and tried to brake my descent. I leant heavily over the axe head, burying it in the slope, but it wouldn't bite. The snow was too loose. I dug my left boot into the slope but it, too, just scraped through the snow.

Then abruptly my feet were in space. I had time to cry out, and claw hopelessly at the snow, before my whole body swung off an edge. I jerked on to the rope and toppled over backwards, spinning in circles from my harness. I was hanging free in space. I could see an ice wall two metres away from me every time I completed a spin. I shone my torch up the wall, following the line of rope, until I could make out the edge I had gone over. The wall was solid ice and steeply overhanging. I could see it dropping below, angled away from me, then snow flurries blocked my view.

There was no chance of Simon hauling me up. It would be suicidal for him to attempt it.

## Simon's account

It had been nearly an hour since Joe had gone over the drop. I was shaking with cold. My grip on the rope kept easing despite my efforts. The thought overwhelmed me that I could not hold the rope or stop the descent. The snow slides and wind and cold were forgotten. I was being pulled off. I slipped a few inches more. Then I thought of the knife. It was in my sack. It took an age to let go a hand and slip the strap off my shoulder, and then repeat it with the other hand. I braced the rope across my thigh and held on to the plate with my right hand as hard as I could. Fumbling at the catches on the rucksack, I could feel the snow slowly giving way beneath me. Panic threatened to swamp me. I felt in the sack, searching desperately for the knife. My hand closed round something smooth and I pulled it out. I put it in my lap. I had already made the decision. There was no other option left to me. The metal blade stuck to my lips when I opened it with my teeth.

I reached down to the rope and then stopped. I had to clear the loose rope twisted round my foot or it would rip me down with it. I carefully cleared it to one side, reached down again, and this time I touched the blade to the rope. It needed no pressure. The taut rope exploded at the touch of the blade and I flew backwards. Leaning back in the snow, I listened to the furious hammering in my temple as I tried to calm my breathing. I was alive, and for the moment that was all I could think about. Where Joe was, or whether he was alive, didn't concern me in the long silence after the cutting. His weight had gone from me. There was only the wind and the avalanches left to me.

When at last I sat up, the slack rope fell from my hips. Had I killed him? I didn't answer the thought, though some urging in the back of my mind told me that I had. I felt numb: freezing cold and shocked into silence, I stared bleakly at the faint torch beam cutting through the swirling snow and felt haunted by its emptiness. Another avalanche swept over me in the darkness. Alone on a storm-swept mountain face, and becoming dangerously cold, I was left with no choice but to forget about Joe until the morning.

Adapted from *Touching the Void* by Joe Simpson, Vintage, 1998.

# Aspects of narrative

## a Viewpoint

Occasionally writers employ the second person when writing narrative, but this is not advisable for exam candidates as it is hard to manage successfully and does not normally fit the composition title. The choice, therefore (if you are given one), is between a first-person and third-person narrator; they both have advantages and disadvantages which candidates need to be aware of before they start their response.

- First-person narrators can only know what they know themselves, and cannot say what other characters are thinking and feeling; they cannot end the story with their death, and it is a cliché to end with their becoming unconscious. On the other hand, an authority and sense of credibility can be conveyed by first-person narration.
- Third-person narration has the advantage of having an all-knowing narrator who can tell us what is going on in the heads of any of the characters (though it is still better to stick to one viewpoint), but it loses the sense of directness which can be conveyed by the use of the first person, who was allegedly involved in the action. The most important thing is that the candidate should make a decision and stick to it, and not switch between different types of narration.

## b Voice

Whether the narrator is first or third person, the voice can be that of a character or witness to an event or sequence of events, and the persona or narrator may adopt a style different from that of the candidate's own style. This can be an effective way of characterising, but candidates must be careful not to adopt a style which includes slang or swearing, or which uses overly simple language and sentence structures, however realistic, because these will be penalised in the assessment of complexity of style and maturity of vocabulary.

## c Characters

It is advisable to have either two or three characters in an exam-length story. More than three makes it hard for them to be adequately characterised and for the reader to distinguish them. It is necessary to explain the relationship between the characters. It is usual to give their name, age (roughly), some clue about their physical appearance and their job – if they have one and and if it is relevant – and their personality. These details allow the reader to picture the characters and engage with them.

## d Storyline

It is not really possible to think of a totally original story, nor do examiners expect it. All writers recycle, with differences of setting and character, a basic set of plots. It is acceptable for candidates to use an idea from a book or film, or to pretend that something which happened to someone else happened to them, provided that the detail is their own and the story has not just been lifted without adaptation or elaboration. Real historical events, as in the case of Text 21, can also be turned into fiction-type narratives. The candidate should not attempt a story which is too long or complex to be delivered in the time available. One event or a short series of events is all that can be managed effectively. A sequence of events should not be linked by 'And then' and treated as being equally important; they should be connected by a chain of cause and effect. Less important occurrences can be skipped over so that the focus is on the major event, which is the one causing the crisis.

## e Tense

Although it is possible to write an effective narrative in the present tense, it is not advisable for exam purposes. So often the candidate forgets they have begun in the present and switches to the past, or keeps switching between the two, since it is unnatural to write about something which is supposed to have already happened in the present, and therefore difficult to remember and sustain. It also limits the narrative viewpoint, and tends to make the language and syntax simple.

## f Structure

The ordering of events is normally, and more safely, chronological. However, an ambitious and capable candidate aiming for top band marks will need to consider using devices such as time lapses, flashbacks, and starting at the end. It is possible not to conclude a story but leave it at the climactic point of greatest tension. This has to be managed carefully so that it is clearly deliberate and does not give the impression that the candidate has run out of time or is avoiding having to provide a resolution. Some writers start with the climax, and then fill in the back story leading to that point, so the story has a circular structure. Another narrative device is to frame the story within another story, which is used for the opening and the ending. For instance, finding a diary many years later, and putting it back in its secret place at the end of the narrative, could frame the reading of it and the story it contains. In any case, characters have to be introduced before their problem can be explained, which precedes the climax, which is followed by the resolution. The climax should come about three quarters of the way through the narrative. Too soon and insufficient tension will have been created; too late and the ending will seem rushed and unprepared for.

## g Openings

First sentences have to grip the reader and engage their curiosity from the beginning. If readers cannot place themselves in a setting they will feel unable to visualise the scene and relate to what is happening. Although the rest of the narrative is likely to have a logical/chronological structure, there is a choice of types of narrative opening:

- the conventional one gives location, surroundings, time, place, weather, season
- one or two main characters can be described as an introduction to an event or action involving them
- a shocking or intriguing opening statement provokes immediate interest
- starting in the middle of an event engages the reader's attention
- starting in the middle of a conversation makes the reader curious about speakers and topic.

## h Description

Narratives need some description as well. Unless the reader can always visualise the setting and the characters they will become disengaged. However, too much description slows down the pace and reduces the tension. Details should be given where they are necessary to create a sense of place and atmosphere, and to convey originality and credibility. For instance, it is better to say exactly what someone is eating or listening to rather than just that they are eating or listening to music.

## i Dialogue

Dialogue should be used sparingly, for dramatic effect, and only for significant exchanges between characters. It is safer for dialogues to be between only two characters at a time, and probably only two of the characters in a short story need to speak directly to each other. It is difficult to manage more than that, or to create distinctive voices for them. When direct speech is used, it must be punctuated and set out correctly, with a new line for every change of speaker, otherwise it becomes impossible for the reader to follow and marks will be lost for inaccuracy.

## j Endings

Endings have to satisfy the reader by being both slightly unpredictable and yet credible in the way they have been led up to. Sometimes a twist can be used to catch the reader off guard and provide humour, irony or surprise, but this must be believable in the context and not a sudden turn of events which is not consistent with the previous characterisation or situation.

# Answers – Unit 21

4  Text 21: viewpoint:

They can be judged to be equally exciting, because both characters are in severe danger which could prove fatal, and although Joe's physical predicament is worse by the end, Simon's terrible decision has left him in an impossible position. A third-person account would not have been as effective as either of these first-person accounts because the reader would not have been able to empathise as much with the intense and agonising thoughts and fears.

6  Text 21: features:

a  Content

Speed of movement, poor visibility, and inability to communicate are always dramatic devices to create suspense. Natural hazards, weather and terrain (*avalanche*), are being used to add to the already dangerous situation. The events are stretched out to add tension, so every movement, however inessential, is mentioned, and the narrative includes the thought processes of the characters to delay the action and intensify the emotional effect.

b  Style

Short sentences create a feeling of panic and provide a change of pace to signify the climax of the story. Alarming vocabulary, such as *agony*, *yell* and *hopelessly*, conveys the feelings of pain and fear.

# Composition – narrative

## Unit 22 Fables, tales and sagas

**Topic outline**

- **Syllabus component:** Paper 3 section 2 question 4; Paper 2 question 2; Paper 4 assignment 2
- **Main skills:** narrative writing
- **Secondary skills:** narrative structure, identifying irony, summarising; editing; analysing writers' effects
- **Outcome:** mini-saga; narrative composition/ coursework type 2; *fable
- **Materials:** animal fables and comic tales; narrative writing structure handout
- **Texts:** Text 22A: The Mouse and the Lion; Text 22B: Animal fables; Text 22C: How the camel got his hump

## Lesson plan

1. Read Text 22A to the class and ask students to think of examples of other fables. Ask them to define a fable and to suggest their purpose. (5)

2. Choose three students to read out Text 22B, one voice for each. Ask students, in pairs, to give each of the tales a suitable moral, based on its ending. (5)

3. Invite students to read out their morals for Text 22B, then compare them with the originals. (5)

4. Read Text 22C to the class. (5)

5. Ask students how the humour has been created in Texts 22B and 22C and to give examples. (5)

6. Ask students, in pairs, to identify the narrative structure of Text 22B. (5)

7. Elicit answers, then give students the handout on narrative writing structure (page 132/CD-ROM).(5)

8. Ask students to think of a film or novel they know which has a strong storyline. Ask them to write a synopsis of half a side, identifying the stages of narrative structure by putting numbers in the margin. (10)

9. Choose students to read out their synopses, while the others guess which book or film they refer to. (5)

10. Write the mini-saga below on the board and ask students to a) define a mini-saga, b) explain its irony, c) give it a title. (5)

*He caught the cat. It was sitting under his van on the road outside his house. Food had been stolen, and rubbish bags torn, making a mess. The cat struggled but he held it fast and strangled it. As he put it in the bin, the fox slipped past unnoticed.*

11. Ask students, in pairs, to reduce Text 22C to a mini-saga. (10)

12. Choose students to read out their versions for comment and comparison. (5)

13. Ask students to write a mini-saga, either their own idea or an adaptation. They must draft and edit their response to become exactly 50 words and consider the structure and ending carefully. Go around, offering advice. (15)

14. Ask for volunteers to read out their mini-sagas (you may wish to collect them for a classroom display or as entries for a school competition). (5)

## Homework task

Write a story of between 350 and 450 words which is a modern version of a fable or fairy tale. (For a coursework piece either a longer version or two separate stories could be written.) The piece could be humorous and/or ironic, and could contain invented words.

## Additional task

Ask students to write a 'Just so' story in the style of Kipling, explaining how another animal got its main characteristic (e.g. 'How the hedgehog got its prickles').

**Text 22A**

# The Mouse and the Lion

*A fable by Aesop*

Once, when a Lion was asleep, a little Mouse began running up and down upon him; this soon wakened the Lion, who placed his huge paw upon him, and opened his big jaws to swallow him.

'Pardon, O King,' cried the little Mouse. 'Forgive me this time; I shall never forget it. Who knows, but I may be able to do you a good turn one of these days.'

The Lion was so tickled at the idea of the Mouse being able to help him that he lifted up his paw and let him go.

Some time afterwards the Lion was caught in a trap, and the hunters who desired to carry him alive to the King tied him to a tree while they went in search of a wagon to carry him on. Just then the little Mouse happened to pass by and, seeing the sad plight of the Lion, went up to him and soon gnawed away the ropes that bound the King of the Beasts and set him free.

'See! Was I not right?' asked the little Mouse.

**Little friends may prove great friends.**

# Text 22B

# Animal fables

## The peacelike mongoose

In cobra country a mongoose was born one day who didn't want to fight cobras or anything else. The word spread from mongoose to mongoose that there was a mongoose who didn't want to fight cobras. If he didn't want to fight anything else, it was his own business, but it was the duty of every mongoose to kill cobras or be killed by cobras.

'Why?' asked the peacelike mongoose, and the word went around that the strange new mongoose was not only pro-cobra and anti-mongoose but intellectually curious and against the ideals and traditions of mongoosism.

'He is crazy,' cried the young mongoose father.
'He is sick,' said his mother.
'He is a coward,' shouted his brothers.
'He is a mongoosexual,' whispered his sisters.

Strangers who had never laid eyes on the peacelike mongoose remembered that they had seen him crawling on his stomach, or trying on cobra hoods, or plotting the violent overthrow of Mongoosia.

'I am trying to use reason and intelligence,' said the strange new mongoose.
'Reason is six-sevenths of treason,' said one of his neighbours.
'Intelligence is what the enemy uses,' said another.

Finally the rumour spread that the mongoose had venom in his sting, like a cobra, and he was tried, convicted by a show of paws, and condemned to banishment.

## The fairly intelligent fly

A large spider in an old house built a beautiful web in which to catch flies. Every time a fly landed on the web and was entangled in it the spider devoured him, so that when another fly came along he would think the web was a safe and quiet place in which to rest.

One day a fairly intelligent fly buzzed around above the web so long without lighting* that the spider appeared and said, 'Come on down.' But the fly was too clever for him and said, 'I never light where I don't see other flies and I don't see any other flies in your house.'

So he flew away until he came to a place where there were a great many other flies. He was about to settle down among them when a bee buzzed up and said, 'Hold it, stupid, that's flypaper. All those flies are trapped.'

'Don't be silly,' said the fly, 'they're dancing.'

So he settled down and became stuck to the flypaper with all the other flies.

*lighting* – settling

## The bears and the monkeys

In a deep forest there lived many bears. They spent the winter sleeping, and the summer playing leap-bear and stealing honey and buns from nearby cottages. One day a fast-talking monkey named Glib showed up and told them that their way of life was bad for bears. 'You are prisoners of pastime,' he said, 'addicted to leap-bear, and slaves of honey and buns.'

The bears were impressed and frightened as Glib went on talking. 'Your forebears have done this to you,' he said. Glib was so glib, glibber than the glibbest monkey they had ever seen before, that the bears believed he must know more than they knew, or than everybody else. But when he left, to tell other species what was the matter with *them*, the bears reverted to their fun and games and their theft of buns and honey.

Their decadence made them bright of eye, light of heart, and quick of paw, and they had a wonderful time, living as bears had always lived, until one day two of Glib's successors appeared, named Monkey Say and Monkey Do. They were even glibber than Glib, and they brought many presents and smiled all the time. 'We have come to liberate you from freedom,' they said. 'This is the New Liberation, twice as good as the old, since there are two of us.'

So each bear was made to wear a collar, and the collars were linked together with chains, and Monkey Do put a ring in the lead bear's nose, and a chain on the lead bear's ring. 'Now you are free to do what I tell you to do,' said Monkey Do.

'Now you are free to say what I want you to say,' said Monkey Say. 'By sparing you the burden of electing your leaders, we save you from the dangers of choice. No more secret ballots, everything open and above board.'

For a long time the bears submitted to their New Liberation, and chanted the slogan the monkeys had taught them: 'Why stand on your own two feet when you can stand on ours?'

Then one day they broke the chains of their new freedom and found their way back to the deep forest and began playing leap-bear again and stealing honey and buns from the nearby cottages. And their laughter and gaiety rang through the forest, birds that had ceased singing began singing again, and all the sounds of the earth were like music.

Source: *Stories and Fables for Our Time* by James Thurber.

# Text 22C

# How the camel got his hump

In the beginning of years, when the world was so new and all, and the Animals were just beginning to work for Man, there was a Camel, and he lived in the middle of a Howling Desert because he did not want to work; and besides, he was a Howler himself. So he ate sticks and thorns and tamarisks and milkweed and prickles, most 'scruciating idle; and when anybody spoke to him he said 'Humph!' Just 'Humph!' and no more.

Presently the Horse came to him on Monday morning, with a saddle on his back and a bit in his mouth, and said, 'Camel, O Camel, come out and trot like the rest of us.'

'Humph!' said the Camel; and the Horse went away and told the Man.

Presently the Dog came to him, with a stick in his mouth, and said, 'Camel, O Camel, come and fetch and carry like the rest of us.'

'Humph!' said the Camel; and the Dog went away and told the Man.

Presently the Ox came to him, with the yoke on his neck and said, 'Camel, O Camel, come and plough like the rest of us.'

'Humph!' said the Camel; and the Ox went away and told the Man.

At the end of the day the Man called the Horse and the Dog and the Ox together, and said, 'Three, O Three, I'm very sorry for you (with the world so new-and-all); but that Humph-thing in the Desert can't work, or he would have been here by now, so I am going to leave him alone, and you must work double-time to make up for it.'

That made the Three very angry (with the world so new-and-all), and they held a palaver, and an *indaba*, and a *punchayet*, and a pow-wow on the edge of the Desert; and the Camel came chewing on milkweed most 'scruciating idle, and laughed at them. Then he said 'Humph!' and went away again.

Presently there came along the Djinn in charge of All Deserts, rolling in a cloud of dust (Djinns always travel that way because it is Magic), and he stopped to palaver and pow-pow with the Three.

'Djinn of All Deserts,' said the Horse, 'is it right for any one to be idle, with the world so new-and-all?'

'Certainly not,' said the Djinn.

'Well,' said the Horse, 'there's a thing in the middle of your Howling Desert (and he's a Howler himself) with a long neck and long legs, and he hasn't done a stroke of work since Monday morning. He won't trot.'

'Whew!' said the Djinn, whistling, 'that's my Camel, for all the gold in Arabia! What does he say about it?'

'He says "Humph!"' said the Dog; 'and he won't fetch and carry.'

'Does he say anything else?'

'Only "Humph!"; and he won't plough,' said the Ox.

'Very good,' said the Djinn. 'I'll humph him if you will kindly wait a minute.'

The Djinn rolled himself up in his dust-cloak, and took a bearing across the desert, and found the Camel most 'scruciatingly idle, looking at his own reflection in a pool of water.

'My long and bubbling friend,' said the Djinn, 'what's this I hear of your doing no work, with the world so new-and-all?'

'Humph!' said the Camel.

The Djinn sat down, with his chin in his hand, and began to think a Great Magic, while the Camel looked at his own reflection in the pool of water.

'You've given the Three extra work ever since Monday morning, all on account of your 'scruciating idleness,' said the Djinn; and he went on thinking Magics, with his chin in his hand.

'Humph!' said the Camel.

'I shouldn't say that again if I were you,' said the Djinn; 'you might say it once too often. Bubbles, I want you to work.'

And the Camel said 'Humph!' again; but no sooner had he said it than he saw his back, that he was so proud of, puffing up and puffing up into a great big lolloping humph.

'Do you see that?' said the Djinn. 'That's your very own humph that you've brought upon your very own self by not working. Today is Thursday, and you've done no work since Monday, when the work began. Now you are going to work.'

'How can I,' said the Camel, 'with this humph on my back?'

'That's made a-purpose,' said the Djinn, 'all because you missed those three days. You will be able to work now for three days without eating, because you can live on your humph; and don't you ever say I never did anything for you. Come out of the Desert and go to the Three, and behave. Humph yourself!'

And the Camel humphed himself, humph and all, and went away to join the Three. And from that day to this the Camel always wears a humph (we call it 'hump' now, not to hurt his feelings); but he has never yet caught up with the three days that he missed at the beginning of the world, and he has never yet learned how to behave.

Source: 'How the Camel got his hump', in *Just So Stories* by Rudyard Kipling.

# Narrative writing structure

| 1 **Setting** |
|---|
| location, surroundings, atmosphere, time of day, week, month, season, weather. |

| 2 **Characters** |
|---|
| Introduce up to three characters by describing their appearance, behaviour and perhaps using direct speech. Make their relationship clear. |

| 3 **Problem** |
|---|
| Create a situation requiring decision or discussion. Build up conflict, perhaps using dialogue. |

| 4 **Climax** |
|---|
| Narrate a series of actions/events, leading to a crisis. Time pressure may be a factor. |

| 5 **Resolution** |
|---|
| Describe the outcome, which may involve an ironic twist. |

# Answers – Unit 22

**1** Definition of a fable:

A fable is a short, succinct allegorical narrative which usually features talking animals to make a moral point about human behaviour memorable and more universally applicable. Fables usually contain an ironic twist at the end, so that someone is taught a lesson by the unexpected outcome.

**3** Text 22B – original morals of the tales:

   **a** Ashes to ashes, and clay to clay, if the enemy doesn't get you your own folks may.

   **b** There is no safety in numbers, or in anything else.

   **c** It is better to have the ring of freedom in your ears than in your nose.

**5** Texts 22B and 22C: comic devices:

Text 22B creates humour by the oddness of the titles, the inversion of clichés, the incongruous mixing of traditional fairytale language with modern idioms and concepts, the ironic endings, the witty morals.

Text 22C creates humour by the use of invented words; misused words (*bubbling* and *lolloping*); silly sounds (*Humph*); the satisfying conclusion of the main character getting his just deserts; the unrealistic (but traditional fairytale) structure of everything happening three times; puns (*forebears*); the anticipated repetition of phrases.

**7** Text 22B: usual narrative structure:
   - setting – time and place
   - main character + other characters and their relationship
   - events / dialogue / conflict creation
   - problem becomes a crisis
   - climax requires a solution
   - resolution

**10** Definition of a mini-saga:

A saga is a long, detailed narrative telling of a series of adventures; by contrast a mini-saga is a minimalistic but complete short story in exactly 50 words, usually dealing with one event. It is likely to have a twist at the end and an implied moral. Structurally it has a clear beginning, middle and end. The final word or phrase is carefully chosen to be significant and placed at the very end for emphasis. Sentences can be of any length, but it should be noted that complex sentences save words, and that a mini-saga can even be one single sentence.

**11** Text 22C as a mini-saga:

A camel refused to work and said only 'Humph!' Three other animals tried in vain to persuade him to work, and were ordered to do extra work because of him. A passing magician punished the camel by giving him a hump so that he could work longer than other animals.

# Coursework – informative/discursive

## Unit 23 Daily lives

**Topic outline**

- **Syllabus component:** Paper 4 assignment 1; Paper 5 or Paper 6 task 1
- **Main skills:** informative writing
- **Secondary skills:** researching; planning; giving a talk
- **Outcome:** informative coursework type 1; individual talk
- **Materials:** magazine monologues; Worksheet for Unit 23: Creating a 'Day in the Life'
- **Texts:** A Day in the Life of … Text 23A: … A pilot; Text 23B: … A storm chaser; Text 23C: … An animal rescuer

## Lesson plan

1 Ask students to read Text 23A. Remind them of VARP in relation to texts (voice, audience, register, purpose). Ask them to discuss in pairs: a) what kind of writing is it? b) who is its voice? c) who is its audience? d) what is its register? and e) what is its purpose? (10)

2 Elicit answers; invite suggestions for jobs which a Day in the Life series might include, and why these would interest readers. (10)

3 Ask students to read Text 23B, then, in pairs, to list the content and style features of the genre, referring to both Texts 23B and 23A (e.g. Content: family, pets, transport, ambitions, memories; Style: first-person, present tense, informative, concise, personal.) (10)

4 Ask students to copy answers to task 3 (see page 143) from board, and discuss the reasons for these features. (5)

5 Ask students to read Text 23C and to check whether it conforms to the checklists on content and style (on page 143). (5)

6 Ask students to make a list of what they do on a typical school day. Discuss the reasons for what they decided to include and what they left out. (10)

7 Give out Worksheet for Unit 23 and ask students to create a character with an important or unusual job. (Discourage them from all choosing the same, gender-stereotyped jobs and suggest they choose one they have a genuine interest in pursuing.) Ask them to complete box 1. (10)

8 Ask students to research or consider their chosen job. (If it is not possible to search on the Internet, they can share ideas, ask you for help, or restrict themselves to a job they already know about.) Stress that an informative piece needs to contain sufficient facts to be convincing. (15)

9 Ask students to complete boxes 2, 3 and 4 of the worksheet, and to check they have covered everything in the content/style lists. (15)

### Homework task

Write your draft of 'A Day in the Life of …', using 500–800 words. You should follow the chronological structure of the day, but insert elements from boxes 3 and 4 of the worksheet at relevant points. Check suitability of style and accuracy before submitting your draft to the teacher for comments. You are advised to word process this coursework piece, and arrange it in columns; if you include an appropriate scanned photograph, it will look more authentic.

### Additional task

Ask students to convert their coursework piece into a talk on a job they would like to do. Ask them questions on it for a Paper 5 assessment, or assess it as a Paper 6 individual task.

# Text 23A

# A Day in the Life of a pilot

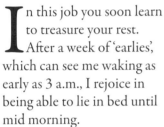

*29-year-old Senior First Officer Theo Fox flies to destinations around Europe for his low-cost airline. He lives in Yorkshire but sees his partner, Francesca, who lives in London, most weekends. His family all live overseas.*

In this job you soon learn to treasure your rest. After a week of 'earlies', which can see me waking as early as 3 a.m., I rejoice in being able to lie in bed until mid morning.

If I'm unlucky I may be called in on a standby duty at no notice because an aircraft has 'gone technical', or a crew member has called in sick or gone out of their allowable duty hours. If you're at the checkout in a supermarket or in the middle of a game of tennis it can be rather inconvenient! On the upside these call-outs can be the most fun kind of work as it may require taking an aircraft somewhere empty, which gives pilots the freedom to have a bit of fun with the aircraft in a way they couldn't with passengers on board!

After recovering from the shock of the alarm clock there follows a quick shower and then breakfast; usually something speedy and unhealthy or wholly unsatisfying, like a breakfast bar or muffin, wolfed down with a cup of tea. Then it's off to the airport, which can be a pleasant experience when gliding along empty morning roads or a complete nightmare at rush hour. The benefit of the uniform though is that people sometimes mistake you for a police officer and give way to you!

Report time is one hour before departure but this can be cutting it a bit fine so I like to arrive with a minimum of an hour and a half. Once through security I go to the crewroom where I'll print off the weather briefs, wind charts and flightplans. Before leaving the crewroom on a crew bus to the aircraft, we tell the cabin crew about flight times, weather and any requirements such as special procedures, aircraft changes, children with birthdays, or VIPs on board. Sometimes I'll ask them to get autographs for me if we're flying a sports team I support!

The airfield apron is a dangerous environment so it's useful to have got the sleep out of your eyes by then so you can monitor reversing vehicles, jetblast from other planes, loud noises and any number of dangerous liquids being sloshed around. Last year I learned that the hard way when some hydraulic fluid ended up in my eyes and the passengers saw their pilot being carried off to hospital by paramedics!

The PF (or Pilot Flying) will brief the departure and set up the navigational aids and engine performance, as well as carrying out security checks and safety equipment checks. Once this is done the passengers are allowed on, while the pilots get their air traffic control clearances and hold their breaths, hoping for no delays. Meeting tight time constraints is essential to the job and there is very little flexibility, so any hiccup has a huge knock-on effect on the day's schedule and increases the pressure on all concerned. If the ground handling agents lose bags or air traffic control causes delays, it is the airline that gets blamed. I have even heard passengers complaining that they won't fly with us again because the flight was too turbulent!

Takeoffs and landings are the areas of highest workload. One of us will fly while the other selects flaps and gear, operates the radio and generally controls the flight deck equipment. Once established in the climb autopilot is usually selected, though if conditions permit we 'hand-fly' as much as possible to keep our skill levels up. If climbing out above the cloud into the morning sun no longer gives you a feeling of freedom and elation it's time to stop flying, as this is what makes it all worthwhile. The natural beauty I get to witness from six miles up makes me feel really privileged, and my photo album is testament to that.

In truth the most challenging part of the flying is generally the landings – which are done manually except in very poor visibility – and there is a lot of professional pride at stake; a heavy landing is a serious embarrassment and earns you mockery from the rest of the crew and occasionally a vocal passenger!

When something goes wrong on approach it is rarely an aircraft fault but usually a sudden wind change or another aircraft blocking the runway. With increased air travel, controllers are under greater pressure to pack arrivals more tightly, so you often have to vacate the runway quickly to allow the aircraft behind to land. Last month we had to abort a landing due to a suspected landing gear fault which turned out to be a trapped fly in a light bulb. Wildlife are often the cause of alarms, from the wasp trapped in the flight deck with us all the way to Malaga to the almost fortnightly bird strikes, and the deer which had to be dodged on the runway in Poland.

Contrary to popular belief pilots are not glorified bus drivers, and the in-flight fuel checks, radio operation, route changes, alternate airfield planning, monitoring the emergency frequency, addressing the passengers, avoiding turbulence, trouble-shooting and setting up the cockpit for arrival keeps us busy and on our toes. A large proportion of our job is planning for the worst, which is why we have six-monthly checks in a simulator to practise dealing with emergencies. Disruptive passengers, medical problems, technical problems and poor weather are common enough to reassure us we are earning our money.

I fly for a low-cost short-haul airline so the pleasures of our exotic destinations are usually limited to a brief trip to duty-free and a stroll in the sun before doing it all again in reverse – sometimes four times a day which can be exhausting. We are permitted to be on duty for about 14 hours, which makes for a long day! But there is no such thing as 'a typical day', which is one of the many attractions of the job for me, though it makes social life and relationships hard to manage. The other downsides are ironing all those shirts, and spending all those hours hunched over my logbook recording it all afterwards – and before I get to see my bed again!

**INTERVIEW BY ROBERT SWAN**

Text 23B

# A Day in the Life of a storm chaser

*The professional photographer and video-maker Mike Hollingshead, 31, exhibits his remarkable images of storms, tornadoes, capped cumulus clouds and all forms of unstable weather on his website, www.extremeinstability.com. He lives alone in Blair, Nebraska, USA.*

The time I get up depends on where the storms are. If I'm driving from Blair, Nebraska to, say, the Texas Panhandle – about 700 miles – I might be up around 4.30 and on the road by 6. I always know where I'm going, because I check the models [weather websites] the night before, and look for areas where different winds are coming together. You need that convergence to get storms going. Most of the action happens from the Panhandle up through Oklahoma, Kansas, Missouri, Nebraska and South Dakota – what they call Tornado Alley.

I might check the latest radar when I wake up, but I don't spend much time on the computer in the morning. I like to get on the road. The Mustang's gas tank's always filled up the night before and I get the gear ready by the door – laptop, cameras, overnight bag, in case I have to stay in a motel, and spare contact lenses. Losing them in a storm wouldn't be too smart!

If there's time, I go to my parents' house and take the dogs for a walk. I've actually missed a couple of great storms because I was taking the dogs out. My parents weren't too crazy about me chasing storms in the early days, but they've kind of got used to it. I've grown up with storms. Up until a couple of years ago I was doing it for fun, but now I've got the website up and running, it's sort of my job.

I always eat my breakfast in the car – maybe a cereal bar and a can of cola. I don't like to eat too much if I'm chasing. It cuts down the times I have to stop. A good day's driving is about six hours to the storm, but I often drive 10 or more. I should take some CDs, but I never get round to it. I just punch around on the radio. I always seem to find classical music – it can really fit the mood.

Lunch doesn't mean anything. I just grab another can and bar when I stop to get some gas – every 300 miles or so. I can do almost 400 on a full tank, but I don't like to let the gauge get below a quarter full.

By noon the satellite images will be coming in, so I'll log on to the internet. I've got a connection from the laptop to my cellphone, which means I can log on from the car. Storm season is usually April till June and, as the day starts to heat up, there'll be a bit more activity.

If you're going to catch a storm, you need to see some powerful cumulus clouds by 3 or 4 in the afternoon. You're looking for capped cumulus clouds. Not the tall, towering ones. You want them a lot flatter. That means things are more unstable. I know what I'm looking for, but I'm not an expert. I did study meteorology at college. Not for long, though. I wanted to be outside with the weather.

Some storms are a couple of miles across and up to 70,000ft high. Really good ones are known as supercells: that's a severe thunderstorm with a constant flow of warm air. They look like solid structures. We call them 'motherships'.

The sound of a tornado is more like a waterfall than anything else, but what can be very loud is hail hitting your car – anything from pea-size to baseball-size. Severe storms can have a constant roll of thunder, too. I mean constant, with no let-up. That can drop off to nothing as soon as a tornado forms, but it can also have the opposite effect, and there'll be a ton of lightning after then.

The feel of a storm is quite sticky, especially in summer, where the dew point can exceed 80F. And in spring, raging surface winds can fill the air with dirt. I've seen debris tossed all over the place. And some of the storms have multiple vortexes – that looks kinda cool.

One of the scariest chases was when I first started out. A tornado in the hills outside Logan, Nebraska. I ended up having to shelter at a gas station and when I came out the town was unrecognisable — it had been ripped apart. Looking back, I wish I hadn't panicked so early. I wish I'd got a better look. That decision still drives me crazy.

I've got some window clamps for the camera, so I just pull up sideways to the storm, wind down the window, stick on the clamp and shoot. I recently got a 10-22 lens – a really wide-angle, so I can get close but still get the whole thing in the frame. Usually the dynamic range of what I'm seeing is a lot more than any camera can handle, so I set the exposure lock on one of the highlights. You need as much light in there as possible.

If I'm close enough to home – up to a six-hour drive – I'll drive back. If not, I'll get a motel. Because I've only been snacking all day, I get pretty hungry. I might stop for a burger or I might end up with a sandwich and a packet of potato chips. I used to download my pictures straight after the chase, but now I tend to wait till the morning, when I can look at them properly.

I dream about storms a lot. Weird, crazy dreams full of panic because my camera won't work or I've taken the wrong road. Sometimes I lie there thinking: 'What am I doing with my life?' I've missed Mother's Day, missed birthdays. I've even missed Christmas Day because of the weather. Then I check the models and I see that there might be something happening in the morning – and I know it'll start all over again.

INTERVIEW BY DANNY SCOTT

Source: *Sunday Times*, 28th October 2007.

# A Day in the Life of *an animal rescuer*

*Cynthia de Gaillac, 43, runs her own animal rescue centre in Gloucestershire, England. Originally of French Huguenot descent, her family have lived in the Forest of Dean since the 17th century. She shares the running of the centre with her husband Claud. They have no children, but a large family of resident animals.*

The alarm goes off at 5.30. Already some of the animals are stirring. If you run an animal rescue centre you inevitably end up with some you can't re-home, so my husband, Claud, and I share our cottage with, at present, 19 assorted creatures of which, today, six are sleeping on our bed. They're all shapes and sizes, ranging from Scooby the ferret, through numerous cats, to Malachite the Abruzzi shepherd and Adamant the pensioned-off greyhound. I hug each of them, get their food, and also see to the ones who sleep elsewhere in the house.

Then I go out and greet the other animals. We've got over 100 at the moment. As I feed them, I always try to make each one feel special, particularly those who've been here the longest, like Otto, a gentle-natured border collie, or Cassius, an Alsatian with huge brown eyes, or Dido, a very patient donkey. I never forget that many of them were abused before we rescued them.

By 7.30, two of my helpers have arrived, so I'll pause to brief them over a coffee and muesli in the kitchen. All of the animal-houses are cleaned daily, including their bedding, which is a huge amount of work.

We have ten acres right in the Forest of Dean, so it's a wonderful place to take the dogs for their walks. Because it's a farming area, we get a lot of border collies – farmers are rarely sentimental if a working dog can't work any more. Sometimes collies just don't seem to understand their job description – Jason preferred to chase the chickens instead of looking after the sheep. Many dogs come from the local pounds when they've been abandoned, and sadly we just don't have space for all of them. We have to take into account whether it will be possible to find them a new home eventually.

I get very involved in my work and I often forget to eat. Claud has to force me to sit down for lunch. We don't eat meat – like so many animal lovers – and we usually grab a sandwich. We are generally interrupted by the phone, often with people reporting animals which will be put down if we don't take them immediately. It's a form of blackmail, but I try not to say no. We will go out a dozen times a week in response to such calls, from individuals or organisations. Some of the animals have some kind of disability. Polly is a lovely, pure-bred Siamese, but she's blind. Sometimes we're offered complete litters because people can't afford to buy pedigree pets any more. They're the easiest to place, of course; everyone prefers a kitten or a pup.

I have a great team of volunteer helpers who run the placement side – Carol who updates the website, Beatrice and Ludovic who check out the new owners, and Mike who drives the van. We also get a lot of the food donated by corporate sponsors, and Philip does a great job co-ordinating them. We have 3 vets who give their services free on a rota, and I can't thank them enough for what they do.

I've always felt this way about animals. I can't explain it. Even as a child I could not bear to see an injured animal or bird. I grew up in the countryside and was always bringing home the creatures I'd rescued. I learned very early that you can't save all of them. Then, when my parents were killed in a horrific car-crash when I was 13, I focused my life entirely on helping those who needed it most.

I left school at 16 to work in an animal shelter and met Claud there. He's a bit older than me, and when he inherited the cottage we knew we could set up our own rescue centre. We called it New Hope because that's what we give our guests.

Claud runs a commercial kennels in part of the grounds, and that's where most of our income comes from, but it means I don't see much of him during our very hectic days. We do make a charge for the adoption of our more 'desirable' guests – puppies and kittens, mostly – but for most of them, we're just glad when somebody wants to take them on, especially the donkeys and the older dogs.

The volunteers leave at around 5.30, but I usually continue on my own, checking that the animals are all ready for the night, especially new arrivals, the traumatised, or those who've been operated on by the vets. Claud and I make a point of sitting down together to eat our only real meal of the day at about 9 pm, and that's when we catch up with what we've each been doing during the day. We usually fall into bed, exhausted, immediately after.

I often lie awake, thinking about an animal I wasn't able to save, or one that has died. But then one of the animals on the bed will creep up and nuzzle me – maybe Giles the sleek grey cat, or Benji the chihuahua – and I'll remember how many we have given a new chance and new hope to. Then I can sleep.

**INTERVIEW BY GEOFFREY COOK**

# Worksheet for Unit 23: 'Creating a Day in the Life'

### 1 Create your biography

Write the answers to the following questions:

What is your name?

___

How old are you?

___

What nationality are you?

___

Where are you living, and who with?

___

What is your job?

Now use the above details to write a brief biographical description, in the third person, like those at the start of the three texts you have looked at (Texts 23A, 23B and 23C).

### 2 Create your daily routine

List the events of your character's day, from getting up to going to bed.

### 3 Create your personality
List the personal details you will include to give yourself a distinctive personality: comment on your taste in meals, transport, music, holidays, hobbies, leisure pursuits.

### 4 Create your philosophy
Give yourself some opinions, aims, beliefs, memories, role models.

# Answers – Unit 23

1. Text 23A: identification:

   a What kind of writing is it? – It is informative non-fiction writing in the genre of an autobiographical monologue.

   b Who is its voice? – The voice appears to be that of the interviewee, but the text was written by the journalist who conducted the interview.

   c Who is its audience? – The readership of the magazine feature series, who are likely to be adults of both genders.

   d What is its register? – It is pretending to be in a spoken, chatty genre yet it is a written text for publication, therefore it has features of both colloquial speech and formal writing.

   e What is its purpose? – Its aim is to inform, but also entertain, readers who are interested in learning about the lives of people in unusual or challenging jobs.

3. Texts 23A and 23B: generic features:
   **Content and style checklists**
   Content:
   - food preferences
   - clothes
   - vehicle/means of transport
   - accommodation
   - family + pets
   - leisure activities
   - holidays
   - thoughts
   - feelings
   - ambitions
   - memories
   - details and statistics and names

   Style:
   - first person
   - present tense
   - variety of sentence structures
   - medium-length paragraphs
   - can include quotation
   - can include exclamations
   - explains technical terms
   - uses standard verb contractions
   - uses *you* not *one* as the impersonal subject pronoun

6. Typical day:

   The events mentioned need to be interesting enough to entertain the reader, but at the same time they should give a faithful picture of the life being described, in order to count as informative rather than fiction writing and convey the reality. Too much reference to dull facts and trivial actions, such as cleaning one's teeth, will make the article tedious and non-specific, but insufficient detail will render the reader unable to empathise with the character and engage with their lifestyle.

# Coursework – informative/discursive

## Unit 24 Hyper-reality

**Topic outline**

- **Syllabus component:** Paper 4 assignment 1; Paper 3 section 2 question 2; Paper 3 section 1; Paper 6 task 2
- **Main skills:** discursive writing
- **Secondary skills:** discussion; summarising; vocabulary building
- **Outcome:** analytical coursework type 1/ argument composition; paired oral activity; *report
- **Materials:** newspaper articles
- **Texts:** Text 24A: Reality check; Text 24B: Murdering innocence

## Lesson plan

1 Discuss what students think about 'reality TV': is/should it be allowed in their country; do they consider it to be entertainment; would they wish to take part; what moral concerns does it raise? (5)

2 Ask students to skim-read Text 24A. (5)

3 Ask students to name the parts of speech and give synonyms for the 20 words in bold. (They may need to consult a thesaurus.) Give answers. (15)

4 Ask students to identify the argument and produce a one-sentence statement to summarise it. (5)

5 Invite students to read out their statements, and comment on them as summaries and as complex sentence structures. (5)

6 Ask students to re-read Text 24A and then, in pairs, to collect and organise material for a dialogue between a psychologist and a TV reality show producer about the selection and treatment of 'housemates'. The characters should each speak five times. (15)

7 Ask pairs to perform their dialogues. (You may assess them as a paired speaking activity for Paper 6 – see CIE website for mark scheme.) (10)

8 Ask students to skim-read Text 24B and to identify the genre and VARP (voice, audience, register, purpose). (5)

9 Ask students to reduce Text 24B to a set of bullet points on the dangers to children of computer games. (10)

10 Put answers on board. Invite students to argue their case if they have different answers. (5)

11 Discuss whether the texts are informative or argumentative (i.e. biased) and how they can tell. Ask students to think of any information or arguments on the other side which have not been made by either of the texts (i.e. to support the view that reality TV and computer games have a positive effect on their viewers/users). Ask students whether their views have changed since their response to task 1? (10)

### Homework task

Either: Draft a piece of coursework in response to the following task: Give your opinion of reality TV programmes and those who produce them, participate in them and watch them.

Or: Write an argument composition answering the following question: 'Reality TV and virtual reality computer games are bad for the health of the individual and of society.' Do you agree with this claim?

### Additional task

Put students in small groups and ask them to devise and conduct a survey of their peers on TV viewing and computer gaming habits. Ask them to write up their findings as a report which draws a conclusion about whether or not these leisure pursuits are harmful to teenagers.

# Reality check

I've had enough, and I'm sure it's not just me. Popular television appears no longer to have any ideas of its own; it merely reacts **gormlessly** to events around itself. Instead of questioning our culture, which is its real job, it merely records the doings of everybody, even if they are **imbeciles**.

Alarmingly, very few people these days appear to understand that actions have consequences. For example, it would be laughable, if it were not so worrying, that our government appears unable to perceive any link between a television programme which **debases** women and a whole generation of girls who therefore believe that by being debased they can achieve celebrity. Nurses, who perform a real service in society, are being tempted to pose for men's magazines by the **lure** of money and parties where they will meet other **nonentities**.

So-called 'reality television' has taken the world by storm. *Big Brother* is now broadcast in almost every country, but its **hapless** participants seem not to realise that they are in reality part of a 'freak show', because they are too stupid to see it. Mostly, they are simply **humiliated** by the experience; sometimes, though, it can kill them. It is believed that his participation in a 'reality' television programme was at least partly responsible for the suicide of a teenager in May 2005, and this was only one of several cases of tragedy linked with this **controversial** genre of programmes. As long ago as 1997 a Swedish man threw himself under a train shortly after his return from a tropical island reality TV show in which he was the first to be voted out. His widow believes that it was fear of humiliation when the programme was broadcast on national television which finally caused him to kill himself.

Those who are already mentally unstable are especially at risk. The television companies claim that they **screen** contestants for pre-exisiting emotional problems which might make them **vulnerable** to being damaged by their experiences, but they have **persistently** failed to **divulge** details of the vetting process they employ, or of what support they offer to participants. The companies state that all the housemates or island castaways have been through a process of assessment and have been declared fit and sufficiently **robust** to cope with the intense pressures of the reality shows, and the programmers also claim that participants are monitored constantly. They are, however, very vague when pressed for details of the **credentials** of the psychologists they use, and some have admitted that they would not allow any adviser to **veto** the participation of a contestant.

The producers of *Big Brother* were also responsible for a programme called *Shattered*, a 'reality' show in which contestants were required to suffer sleep deprivation over a period of days, the winner being the one who slept least. This led to **trenchant** criticism from professional researchers in the field of sleep research at universities, and subsequently advisers to the same show admitted that although they had recommended a ban on the use of electric shocks, it had been ignored.

Producers will inevitably prefer to use characters whose weaknesses and psychological state **render** them liable to **succumb** to stress or to engage in conflict in the situations which the TV company **concocts**. The companies fall back upon the **contention** that no-one is forced to participate, and that all are free to leave at any time; independent consultants, however, believe that the sums of money involved prevent participants from giving truly informed consent to what they will be exposed to, and those who are, objectively, least suited to the stresses of appearing on 'reality' TV are precisely the people whose vulnerabilities and instability make the programmes irresistible to an undiscerning audience, and such profitable ventures for their makers.

# Text 24B

# Murdering *innocence*

An article in a leading medical journal has confirmed what many of us suspected: violence on television and in computer games does make children more aggressive and fearful. Boys are more susceptible than girls, and doctors now say that exposing children to such images is tantamount to 'emotional maltreatment'.

Children up to five are most affected by the images, then children up to 11. By the time they reach adolescence the impact of these disturbing images is lessened, presumably because people's emotional responses have by then been bludgeoned out of recognition. We seem to have a mental block when it comes to violence in general and violent computer games in particular. Parents are happy to go out and buy their children Grand Theft Auto and pop it into their Christmas stocking. It is the fastest selling computer game in history; after its launch date it sold 1m copies in nine days. In the game you are a sociopath running amok in a thinly disguised Los Angeles, San Francisco and Las Vegas, avenging the murder of your mother. You slaughter, maim and rob. The graphics are brilliant, which is to say hyper-realistic.

I think many parents assume that benign-sounding computer games are just that: set in reassuringly cartoonish imaginary worlds with no whiff of reality about them. Grand Theft Auto does not fall into this category. Worse, it is knowingly blackly funny in parts, which is fine if you are an adult but dangerously alluring if you are a child. Playing a game involving random slaughter is one thing: being invited to have a good laugh about it is quite another. It has made its way into thousands of little boys' bedrooms. So has another especially unpleasant game, Manhunt, blamed by a father for the murder of his 14-year-old son by his friend with a knife and claw hammer. The father claimed that the game acted as an 'instruction manual' for his son's 50 separate injuries, and he is suing the manufacturer.

These games are addictive and provide entire alternative worlds for bored and curious children. Exploring these worlds and their many levels can take weeks or months, weeks or months spent alone in the creepy glow of the console screen, inhabiting a universe where everyone involved is brutalised and brutalising. Part of our negligence when it comes to the issue of violence is that we think it comes with the territory as parents of boys. We don't necessarily like it, but we detach ourselves from what such games mean and from the question of the impact they might have. Increasingly the home computer has replaced the television as our favourite unpaid babysitter. Parents should, however, be aware that allowing children access to these games is a form of abuse and that the reason this happens is parental laziness. There is no point in banning games such as Grand Theft Auto. All the legislation in the world won't stop young boys playing totally inappropriate games – only their parents can do that. And the sad truth is that most parents can't be bothered.

Adapted from 'The kiddie killing fields' by India Knight, *Sunday Times*, 20th February 2005.

# Answers – Unit 24

**3**   Text 24A: parts of speech and synonyms:

| | |
|---|---|
| **gormlessly** – adverb – *stupidly* | **persistently** – adverb – *continuously* |
| **imbeciles** – noun – *idiots* | **divulge** – verb – *reveal* |
| **debases** – verb – *degrades* | **robust** – adjective – *strong* |
| **lure** – noun – *attraction* | **credentials** – noun – *experience* |
| **nonentities** – noun – *insignificant people* | **veto** – verb – *refuse* |
| **hapless** – adjective – *unfortunate* | **trenchant** – adjective – *severe* |
| **humiliated** – verb – *demeaned/degraded* | **render** – verb – *make* |
| **controversial** – adjective – *debatable* | **succumb** – verb – *submit* |
| **screen** – verb – *test* | **concocts** – verb – *invents* |
| **vulnerable** – adjective – *susceptible* | **contention** – noun – *claim* |

**4**   Text 24A: one-sentence summary of the argument:

Text 24A is arguing that popular television holds up for admiration mindless spectacles of human behaviour, which are damaging to many of those who take part – who have been enticed by promises of fame and wealth – when it should be questioning the validity of reality TV programmes but chooses not to do so, because they boost viewing figures by taking advantage of those with personality disorders and putting them into abusive situations without protection so that they show signs of extreme, and therefore entertaining, behaviour.

**8**   Text 24B: characteristics:

**Genre** – newspaper article commenting on a current social issue

**Voice** – the journalist, who is also a concerned parent

**Audience** – reasonably well-off, reasonably well-educated adults and fellow parents, especially of boys (readers of the newspaper)

**Register** – the title of the article is polemical, i.e. deliberately provocative about the responsibilities of parents (e.g. *mental block*, *can't be bothered*)

**Purpose** – to persuade parents to take an interest in the computer games their children play and stop them playing inappropriate ones

**9**   Text 24B: dangers of computer games:
- make children more aggressive and fearful
- deaden emotional responses
- encourage the view that violence and crime are harmless
- influence of over-realistic graphics
- allure of adult humour
- cause of children murdering each other
- addictiveness of games over a long period
- brutalising effect
- encourage acceptance that boys are inevitably violent
- cause parents to believe children are being safely looked after
- encourage parental laziness and ignorance

# Coursework – descriptive/narrative

## Unit 25 Seeing the future

**Topic outline**

- **Syllabus component:** Paper 4 assignment 2; Paper 3 section 2 question 4; Paper 6 task 1; Paper 6 task 3
- **Main skills:** narrative writing; descriptive writing
- **Secondary skills:** imagining; supporting views; discussion
- **Outcome:** imaginative blog entry; narrative coursework/narrative composition; group discussion; *individual talk
- **Materials:** short story opening; picture of futuristic city
- **Texts:** Text 25: August 4, 2026; Picture 25: City of the future

## Lesson plan

1. Ask students how they think the future might be different from the present. Ask them to make a spider diagram which includes ideas about the following: buildings, vehicles, clothing, education, leisure. (5)

2. Ask students to imagine they have just visited their country 50 years from now. Ask them to write a blog entry of one page describing what they have seen and their feelings about how things have changed. (15)

3. Invite students to read extracts from their blogs to the class. (5)

4. Discuss the concept of a time capsule: who makes them, when, why, and what kind of things are put into them. Collect ideas for contents on board. (10)

5. Ask the class to imagine they are going to make a time capsule to mark a school or community anniversary. Allow one suggestion per student for what to put in it. Ask them to prepare a one-paragraph description of their object and justify why it should be included. (10)

6. Ask students to read out their choices and rationales. Vote on which ones to accept. (10)

7. Read out Text 25 while students imagine the scene. (5)

8. Ask students what they can infer from the opening of the short story about a) life in 2026 in California, b) what happened in the past, and c) what is going to happen next. (5)

9. Ask students to look at Picture 25 (print handout or show projection from CD-ROM), and to collect phrases and images which effectively describe it. (A thesaurus may be useful.) (5)

10. Invite students to read their phrases. Collect the best on the board. (5)

11. Ask students to use ideas from Text 25, Picture 25, and the spider diagram for task 1, in a small group discussion of 'City life 50 years from now'. Ensure that it covers architecture, transport, domestic living and the appearance of the inhabitants. (This discussion can be assessed for Paper 6 task 3 – see CIE website for mark scheme.) (10)

12. Ask students to brainstorm ideas for their own futuristic story, beginning at breakfast time on a day in 2060. They should decide where the story is going and how it will end, and give it a title. (5)

## Homework task

Using your plan for task 12, write either the draft of a coursework assignment (500–800 words) or a narrative composition (350–450 words); in either case include descriptive detail to create setting and atmosphere, and to engage the reader.

## Additional task

Ask students to write a speech to deliver to the class, entitled either 'Life can only get better' or 'Life can only get worse'. They should describe their vision of life in their country by the end of their lifetime, using ideas from their blog entry for task 2, and reflect on whether or not this represents progress.

# Text 25

# August 4, 2026

In the living room the voice-clock sang. 'Tick-tock, seven o'clock, time to get up, time to get up, seven o'clock!' As if it were afraid that nobody would. The morning house lay empty. The clock ticked on, repeating and repeating its sounds into the emptiness.

'Seven-nine, breakfast time, seven-nine!'

In the kitchen the breakfast stove gave a hissing sigh and ejected from its warm interior eight pieces of perfectly browned toast, eight eggs sunnyside up, sixteen slices of bacon, two coffees, and two cool glasses of milk.

'Today is August 4, 2026,' said a second voice from the kitchen ceiling, 'in the city of Allendale, California.' It repeated the date three times for memory's sake. 'Today is Mr Featherstone's birthday. Today is the anniversary of Tilita's marriage. Insurance is payable, as are the water, gas, and light bills.'

Somewhere in the walls, relays clicked, memory tapes glided under electric eyes.

'Eight-one, tick-tock, eight-one o'clock, off to school, off to work, run, run, eight-one!'

But no doors slammed, no carpets took the soft tread of rubber heels. It was raining outside. The weather box on the front door sang quietly: 'Rain, rain, go away; rubbers, raincoats for today …' And the rain tapped on the empty house, echoing.

Outside the garage chimed and lifted its door to reveal the waiting car. After a long wait the door swung down again.

At eight-thirty the eggs were shriveled and the toast was like stone. An aluminum wedge scraped them into the sink, where hot water whirled them down a metal throat which digested and flushed them away to the distant sea. The dirty dishes were dropped into a hot washer and emerged twinkling dry.

'Nine-fifteen,' sang the clock, 'time to clean.'

Out of warrens in the wall, tiny robot mice darted. The rooms were acrawl with the small cleaning animals, all rubber and metal. They thudded against chairs, whirling their mustached runners, kneading the rug nap, sucking gently at hidden dust. Then, like mysterious invaders, they popped into their burrows. Their pink electric eyes faded. The house was clean.

Ten o'clock. The sun came out from behind the rain. The house stood alone in a city of rubble and ashes. This was the one house left standing. At night the ruined city gave off a radioactive glow which could be seen for miles.

**Source:** 'There will come soft rains' by Ray Bradbury, in *The Martian Chronicles*, HarperVoyager, 1995.

**Note:** American spelling is used throughout this text.

## Picture 25: City of the future

# Answers – Unit 25

**4** Time capsules:

They contain evidence of untampered truth, unlike historical data compiled by journalists or artists. An object is itself and cannot lie. A time capsule addresses eternity. It preserves the present for the future and embodies a hope that there will be one, and people to open it. The kinds of things which could be included are: recordings on devices such as CDs and DVDs (though the technology to play them may not exist in the future), photographs, weapons, menus, price lists (e.g. house prices), can of petrol, sweets/drinks, magazines, trophies and medals, articles of clothing. These all indicate the way we live now, our concerns, our pleasures and our values; some will amaze and baffle our descendants – though it's impossible to know which ones.

**8** Text 25: inferences:

   **a** The climate has not changed, food has not changed, but the sophistication of domestic appliances has. Machines are relied upon to inform humans of times, dates, tasks, controlled to the exact minute. Doing things exactly on time seems to have become very important, and routine governs everything. We can infer from the list of breakfast items that the family consisted of the regular two adults and two children. Names may have evolved, as *Tilita* is unusual. Children still go to school and adults still go to work outside the home, by car. Household bills still have to be paid. There is lots of noise of a mindless singsong variety, based on rhyme and repetition, as though adults are being treated as infants by the machines and robots, which are programmed to perform all domestic tasks.

   **b** There has been a nuclear explosion, the city has been destroyed, and presumably all of its inhabitants. In any case, the area is too polluted by radiation for humans to live in or visit the city any more.

   **c** The question is how long a house can go on running itself without human existence, and what would cause an eventual breakdown of the system.

(Bear in mind that this story was written in 1950 and some of these things may have already changed, e.g. going off to work is now less common as so many people tele-work from home. We have already far more electric and electronic gadgets and are more dependent on machinery and technology than was conceivable in the mid 20th century, even in the USA, when a hoover was considered a luxury and dishwashers were almost unheard of.)

# Coursework – descriptive/narrative

## Unit 26 Famous face

**Topic outline**

- **Syllabus component:** Paper 4 assignment 2
- **Main skills:** descriptive writing; responding imaginatively
- **Secondary skills:** narrative writing; monologues; inference
- **Outcome:** descriptive coursework type 2; monologue
- **Materials:** images
- **Texts:** Slideshow 26: Mona Lisa (see CD-ROM)

## Lesson plan

1 Ask students what comes into their minds when they hear the name 'Mona Lisa'. Make a spider diagram on the board. (5)

2 Show the slideshow (12 slides) and ask students to take notes on anything they find interesting or wish to ask about. Leave slide 2 on the screen and discuss the slideshow as a class. (15)

3 Ask students to look closely at the painting and make notes on the following:

   a  a detailed description of her face, using imagery

   b  a description of the life she leads

   c  a description of what she is thinking and feeling while she is sitting for the portrait. (15)

4 Invite responses and ask students to explain and justify them. (10)

5 Ask students to design their own version of the painting, considering clothing, background and expression. (Maybe they see her as a cartoon or even an abstract.) Ask students to make a rough sketch on a sheet of blank paper. Go around, prompting ideas. (5)

6 Invite students to show their sketches and to explain the changes they have made. (10)

7 Ask students to imagine what Mona Lisa would say to a crowd of people looking at her. Ask them to write a monologue of about one side in her voice. (15)

8 Invite students to read out their monologues for comment. (5)

9 Ask students to plan an imaginative personal response to the painting, using ideas from the spider diagram in task 1, the information in the slideshow, and their response to tasks 3, 5 and 7. They should consider the painting's content, history, fame; its enigmatic smile; its power over viewers; its political significance; its inspiration to the art world; its commercial exploitation. (10)

## Homework task

Write the draft of a coursework piece, using your plan from task 9, with the title: 'The most famous face in the world'. You need to adopt a structure for the piece, as even imaginative writing needs to have coherence and linkage.

## Additional tasks

a  Show students a picture of a scene in a painting which contains several characters engaged in an activity. Ask them to write a narrative which leads up to and explains what they are doing, and which includes dialogue between the characters.

b  Play a piece of instrumental music and ask students to record their 'stream of consciousness' while they are listening. It may be a descriptive or a narrative response.

# Slideshow 26 Mona Lisa

### 1
*La Gioconda:*
Renaissance woman to modern icon

### 2

### 3 Mona Lisa, La Gioconda
- Arguably the most famous painting in the world, it was begun by Leonardo da Vinci in 1503 but was not completed until shortly before his death.
- The subject is Lisa Gherardini, wife of Francesco del Giocondo, a wealthy Florentine silk merchant, hence the name 'La Gioconda'.
- Leonardo was living in Paris at the time he finished the painting, and it's home has been the Louvre gallery since then.
- The painting was stolen in 1911. It was found in Florence two years later.

### 4 Leonardo da Vinci
- Born 1452 in Vinci near Florence, he was the illegitimate son of a public notary.
- He moved to Florence at the age of 17 and was apprenticed to the celebrated painter Andrea del Verrocchio.
- He became a celebrated polymath and 'Renaissance Man', a brilliant artist, sculptor, scientist, engineer and inventor.
- He worked in Florence, Milan and Rome before moving to Paris in 1516.
- Leonardo died in 1519 and was buried in France, his adopted home.

### 5 Mona Lisa's smile
- La Gioconda is painted in Leonardo's 'sfumato' style, in which the colours dissolve into each other, creating a softening of outlines and a subtle texture.
- The expression on Mona Lisa's face is often described as 'enigmatic' – literally, concealing a mystery.

### 6
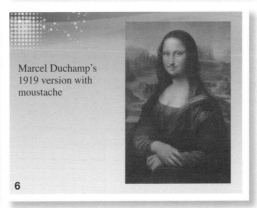

Marcel Duchamp's 1919 version with moustache

### 7
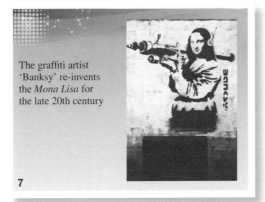

The graffiti artist 'Banksy' re-invents the *Mona Lisa* for the late 20th century

### 8
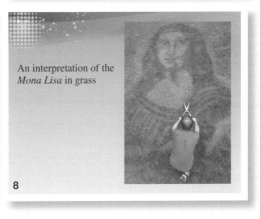

An interpretation of the *Mona Lisa* in grass

Unit 26 ○ **Famous face**

An interpretation of the *Mona Lisa* in Lego®

9

The *Mona Lisa* made out of slices of toast

10

The unveiling of the *Mona Lisa* in New York, 1961

11

## How the *Mona Lisa* came to 'Camelot'

'Mona mania' changed the world in 1962 when the wife of the then president of the United States, Jackie Kennedy, received on December 19th the Christmas gift she had long dreamt of: the *Mona Lisa*. The painting was brought by ship from France, the first time La Gioconda had ever left the Louvre art gallery in Paris on loan, and she was regarded by many in the art world as too fragile to travel, since the old lady was 500 years old and she needed a constant temperature and humidity. She was to be on holiday for three months to cement a Franco-American political alliance against communism. Two million people in Washington and New York queued to visit Mona Lisa. She was heralded as a symbol of freedom, but 8 months later president John F. Kennedy was assassinated.

12

# Coursework – evaluation of argument

## Unit 27 Self-esteem v. self-control

**Topic outline**

- **Syllabus component:** Paper 4 assignment 3; Paper 3 section 1; Paper 6 task 3
- **Main skills:** evaluative writing
- **Secondary skills:** forming opinions; summarising; identifying rhetorical devices; defending and refuting arguments; group discussion
- **Outcome:** evaluative coursework type 3; *directed writing; *Paper 6 group discussion
- **Materials:** argument texts (book and newspaper article)
- **Texts:** Text 27A: All about me; Text 27B: Punishment, not praise

## Lesson plan

1. Ask students to define and give their views on the concept of self-esteem, giving examples of personal experiences, and suggesting people they associate with having a high degree of it; for and against arguments. Collect ideas in two columns, for and against, on board. (10)

2. Ask students to read Text 27A for gist. Then ask them to re-read Text 27A, highlighting the separate arguments. (10)

3. Ask students to write a list of the arguments used in the article, expressing them concisely and in their own words. (5)

4. Invite students to read out their lists and compare others with their own, disputing the inclusion, omission or interpretation of points if necessary. (5)

5. Ask students to read Text 27B for gist and then re-read to identify and underline, in pairs, the rhetorical devices being used. (5)

6. Go through the devices, asking for explanations of how they manipulate the reader in each case. (5)

7. Ask students to select ideas from Text 27B to use in a small-group discussion on self-esteem. (10)

8. Ask groups to conduct their discussions, referring to the arguments used in Texts 27A and 27B, and the columns on the board. Go around class, either to prompt or to assess the discussions as a Paper 6 group activity. (15)

9. Ask students to consider all the written material and discussion and to formulate a statement summarising their own response to the question 'Is self-esteem overestimated?', giving the main evidence on which their opinion is based. (5)

10. Invite students to read out their position statements and comment on them as arguments. (5)

11. Ask students to plan their coursework assignment, which is an evaluative analysis of the arguments used in Text 27A. They should list the references they will make to the text, and how they will support or refute those claims in the light of their own views and those of others (including Text 27B). They should comment in detail on at least five claims made in Text 27A, and draw a conclusion about the effectiveness of the argument overall. (15)

## Homework task

Either: Write the draft of your coursework assignment using between 500 and 800 words. Check your draft carefully before submission for sequencing and linking of ideas, and for variety, complexity and accuracy of expression.

Or: Write an argumentative composition on the title 'Self-esteem and self-confidence are necessary to success. Do you agree?'

## Additional task

Write to the author of Text 27B and explain why, as a teenager and student, you do or do not agree with his opinion, giving detailed support for your view.

# Text 27A

# All about ME

From the 1970s onwards, a quiet revolution took place in American education – and, arguably to a lesser extent, in British education also. Whereas life in high schools in America used to centre upon Grade Point Averages and Honour Rolls, where every student knew his or her place in the academic hierarchy, the advocates of the so-called 'Self-Esteem' movement threw all this aside in order that all children should 'feel good about themselves'. They argued that failing or getting a low grade was an unpleasant experience – so it should be banned. Many high schools taught courses in Self-Esteem. Teachers were told not to mark or evaluate students' work; some went so far as to give every piece of work an A, and banned the use of red pens by teachers in case they offended the students. Honour rolls were abolished, and the fiction was maintained that all students were equally talented and were high achievers, no matter how little they did. An especially worrying feature of the more extreme versions of the Self-Esteem movement was the idea that correct spelling was an unreasonable tyranny, so children should be praised for spelling words in any way they fancied. Parents, too, were sucked in, and told that they should praise their children, all the time, whatever they did. The development of 'individuality' was more important than effective socialisation.

Since the turn of the century, a reaction has, not surprisingly, set in – occasioned not least by the mis-match between what the schools (and parents) were saying and the reality of life after school. Universities and employers refused to buy in to this nonsense; universities needed students with knowledge, skills and suitable attitudes – and so continued to select using real criteria – and employers needed employees who were capable of doing the job. Both of these key groups found that students who had never been taught the concept of standards, and thought that an A grade could be earned by writing their name (whether spelled correctly or not), were of no use to them at all.

The attack came from a number of fronts. Roy Baumeister, a leading psychologist who conducted an extensive review of the phenomenon, found that the self-esteem programmes did not actually result in any of the benefits claimed by their exponents: students did not achieve better grades (in any real sense, as opposed to inflated grades given for nothing); nor did the programmes reduce violence, cheating or anti-social behaviour. On the contrary, he found that those who had been exposed to the programmes were often more violent and more likely to cheat than those who had not; they were self-centred and cynical about the whole educational process, because they knew that the praise and grades they received were meaningless. Baumeister concluded, 'After all these years, I'm sorry to say, my recommendation is this: forget about self-esteem and concentrate more on self-control and self-discipline.'

American social commentator Jean M. Twenge coined the phrase 'Generation Me' in her 2006 book of the same name to describe a phenomenon which she observed developing in the society around her. Under the influence of the so-called 'Self-Esteem Movement', parents were coming under pressure not to set any standards of behaviour for their children; rather than punishing them if they did wrong, parents, it was argued, should boost their children's 'self-esteem' by praising them for anything they did. The consequence of this, she claimed, was a generation of self-obsessed children who had no standards against which to judge their behaviour or achievements and who were, ironically, deprived of the key learning experience of being valued for something they had worked for and truly accomplished.

Most crucially, Twenge argued, the 'Self-Esteem' movement was anti-educational because students could not understand the value of anything. They were not being prepared in any way for life. Protecting them from criticism in childhood meant that they were completely unprepared for it, and unable to deal with it, when it inevitably came in adult life.

Twenge also argued that the movement was fundamentally misguided and based upon false premises. Whilst it is true that many American (and British) schools in the 1950s and 1960s were obsessed with grades and hierarchies at the expense of individual development, what was really needed to counteract this was the educational philosophy increasingly adopted in Europe over the past 30 years: that every child matters, every child has ability in some field, and that the purpose of education is to help every child to achieve his or her potential, whether it be in – academic work, sport, drama, community service or anything else. It was also important that children should learn from their mistakes (not have them reinforced), and should receive constructive feedback to help them to improve their performance. Children cannot evaluate either conduct or achievement unless they understand and accept the objective standards applied by trusted adults – such as parents and teachers. An essential element of 'education for life' is to develop empathy with and respect for others. Psychologists have found that those whose self-esteem is artificially induced are often 'narcissistic' – obsessed with themselves, devoid of secure judgement and incapable of appreciating the viewpoint or needs of others.

It is also vital that children should be helped to establish realistic expectations, and Twenge is especially scornful of those who tell children to 'follow their dream' – that they can have anything if they want it enough – because it simply is not true in the real world. What children need to be told, if they are to develop into true and effective individuals, is that they are valued for themselves and for their talents, whatever they may be, but they need to work hard to achieve goals and career success. As Baumeister puts it, self-control and self-discipline deliver results: self-esteem delivers a cruel illusion.

# Text 27B

# Punishment, not praise

Well, all I can say is that I hope you are counting. How many times have you praised your out-of-control little monster today? If government advice on school discipline applies, as logically it should, in the home, then parents across the country will need to keep a constant check on their response to the undesirable behaviour of their offspring. Five to one is the ratio of praise to punishment, ladies and gentlemen. Criticise rarely; keep punishment to the barest possible minimum; praise and reward however monstrous the offence. Follow the latest ministerial guidance and your children will understand the difference between right and wrong and learn to act with adult responsibility in every circumstance. Just pat them on the head and tell them how wonderful they are.

Of course it is important to praise children, and, looking back as a parent and a teacher, I would be the first to admit that I probably did not praise enough. Few of us do. A little recognition goes a long way, and everyone who has responsibility for children needs to remind themselves of this commonsense truth. To that extent the government's advice is sensible. How, though, did it come up with this 5:1 statistic? This is a finger-in-the-wind generalisation that is meaningless in any specific circumstance.

Meaningless, and, what is worse, insidious. Yes, children should be praised when they do something good. To suggest it is somehow wrong to punish them when they do something bad, or, more ridiculous still, actually to reward unacceptable behaviour, is to send a message that is not so much stupid as dangerous. Children need boundaries. They need to know what they are allowed to do and what they are not allowed to do. And they need to understand that if they choose to break the rules, the consequences are unpleasant.

Talk to any head teacher who has turned round a failing school. The first thing they will tell you is that they had to deal with pupils who would not accept the conventions of normal schooling. Without order, nothing. It is not rocket science. Punctuality, attendance, uniform, behaviour; the heads would make their expectations clear, and they would ensure everyone knew what would happen to those who stepped out of line. Good behaviour would be praised and bad behaviour would be punished. Make the rules clear and apply them fairly. Children know where they are and teachers can start teaching again.

Source: Chris Woodhead, *Sunday Times*, 15th April 2007.

# Answers – Unit 27

**3** Text 27A: list of arguments:
- American teachers have stopped correcting children's work as they believe criticism damages their self-esteem.
- Psychologists are warning that these trends have not only made no improvement to grades and behaviour but have increased the likelihood of cheating and violence in schools.
- Psychologists claim that what is needed is not more self-esteem but more self-discipline.
- Attempting a challenge is more character-building and rewarding than not trying at all or being allowed to give up because of laziness or fear of failure.
- Failing can be a positive experience.
- All children are good at something.
- True self-worth comes from learning new skills and applying one's talents, not from being told you are wonderful simply because you exist.
- Self-control can achieve the ends which self-esteem has failed to bring about, and equips a child to cope with adversity and be protected from misery.
- Children sheltered from failure and shielded from challenges cannot deal with life's disappointments.
- Competition is necessary to stretch children to perform their best.
- Self-esteem is the easier option and therefore attractive to students and teachers.
- Rewards should only be for achievement, not for doing nothing, otherwise children become cynical.
- It is not fair to tell children they can do and be anything they want, because it isn't true.
- Hard work is necessary for getting somewhere in life.
- Self-esteem fosters unrealistic expectations.

**6** Text 27B: list of rhetorical devices and their effects:

**colloquialisms** – to create conversational effect and invite reader trust (e.g *Well* and *Yes*)

**addressing reader as 'you'** – for intimacy and presupposition that the reader will agree

**rhetorical questions** – to engage and involve reader

**triple structures** – to make utterances memorable and effective

**sarcasm** – for mockery of opponents so that reader will not wish to identify with them

**imperatives** – to sound authoritative and superior (e.g. *Follow*, *Talk*)

**repetition of words** – for emphasis (e.g. *meaningless*, *need*)

**short categorical sentences** – to give the impression that there can be no counter argument

**insults** – to ridicule opponents (*little monster*, *stupid*)

**non-sentences** – to make the sentiment sound decisive (e.g. *Without order, nothing.*)

**modern idiom** – to show the writer is up to date (e.g. *It is not rocket science*)

**lists** – to give the impression that the writer is well informed

**antithesis** – to make it seem a simple two-sided issue

**admission of fallibility** – to make what follows seem honest

# Coursework – evaluation of argument

## Unit 28 Science or sentiment?

**Topic outline**

- **Syllabus component:** Paper 4 assignment 3; Paper 3 section 1; Paper 3 section 2 question 1; Paper 6 task 1
- **Main skills:** evaluating argument; argumentative writing
- **Secondary skills:** detecting bias; persuasive devices; directed writing
- **Outcome:** evaluative coursework type 3; website appeal; debate speech; *Paper 6 individual talk
- **Materials:** newspaper articles
- **Texts:** Text 28A: A helping hand; Text 28B: Do animals have emotions?

## Lesson plan

1. Ask students to read Text 28A and say whether or not they are convinced by the argument that dolphins are altruistic, citing the point which convinced them either way. (5)

2. Ask students to re-read Text 28A and, in pairs, to highlight in two different colours the facts and the opinions. (10)

3. Elicit answers and put them on board in two columns. (5)

4. Ask students to read Text 28B and say whether or not they are convinced by the argument that animals experience human-type emotions. Invite responses as before. (5)

5. Ask students to study Text 28B and, in pairs, to highlight in two different colours the facts and the opinions. (10)

6. Elicit answers and put them on board in two columns. (5)

7. Ask students to plan an appeal letter of one page which asks for donations to help protect either dolphins or apes, keeping VARP in mind (voice, audience, register, purpose). (10)

8. Ask students to write the appeal, using persuasive devices. (15)

9. Ask students to check each other's appeals for accuracy of spelling, punctuation and grammar. Collect them to assess as a directed writing task. (5)

10. Ask students to plan and draft a debate speech for or against the motion 'Animals have instinct not intelligence.' They should use material from Texts 28A and 28B, and their own ideas and experiences. They should also try to anticipate and refute the arguments the other side might use. (20)

## Homework task

Either: Write a draft of a coursework piece which evaluates the arguments presented in Text 28B, using material from Text 28A to support or refute them.

Or: Write an argumentative composition entitled 'Do you believe that animals feel emotion?', using your draft from task 10 as a plan.

## Additional task

Ask students to turn their draft debate speech into a final version and to deliver their speeches for the class to evaluate in terms of both range and strength of argument (you may also assess the speeches as a Paper 6 type 1 task).

# Text 28A

# A helping hand
The author is Emeritus Professor of Natural History at Edinburgh

Undoubtedly, it must have been an extraordinary sight to behold – one great beast of the sea coming to the aid of another. Like most people, I was both fascinated and rather touched by yesterday's story of a dolphin coming to the aid of a pygmy sperm whale and her calf which had repeatedly beached themselves on a drying sandbank.

According to eye-witness accounts from the North Island of New Zealand, local wildlife volunteers had had no success in persuading the whales to return to deeper waters. With time fast running out, it was only when Moko – a female dolphin apparently well-known in those parts – bobbed up and started calling to the whales that mother and calf were finally persuaded to move out to safety and the open sea.

This would be one of the most amazing cases of inter-species cooperation ever recorded, especially as from Moko's perspective it appears to be an entirely selfless act. By and large, adult animals rarely do anything unless there is something in it for them. When they do, however, it's generally because something has gone awry with their sense of self. Indeed, it is this behaviour that usually lies behind the images that we all love to look at – kittens that are being raised by a dog; the mouse that is best friends with a cat; or, in one extraordinary case I've heard of, a lioness raising an orphaned gazelle. There is also a story of a crow lovingly feeding a kitten.

As someone who has studied animal behaviour for many years, I know that there is often a fairly straightforward explanation behind these incredibly heart-warming images. It is that one or other of the animals involved has simply got confused about its identity. This process of learning identity is called 'imprinting' by animal behaviourists and normally takes place when the animal is growing up. Sometimes, however, this development goes wrong. […] Many scientists will tell you that faulty imprinting lies behind all apparent examples of inter-species cooperation. It may well be that with Moko the dolphin it was a case of mistaken identity.

One of the main debates that rages endlessly in animal behaviour circles is about what sort of 'sense of self' animals have. In other words, would Moko the dolphin know that she was a dolphin and would she know that some animals that look quite like dolphins – such as pygmy sperm whales, for example – aren't always dolphins? It may be that Moko actually mistook the whales for dolphins, and came to their aid accordingly. But I'm retaining an open mind; coastal dolphins such as Moko have a long and noble reputation for coming to the aid of distressed mammals

– including human swimmers who have got into difficulties.

There are many other amazing examples of co-operation to be found in the animal kingdom. I am still fascinated by reliable evidence gathered from the shores of Lake Tanganyika, where the young of a troop of visiting chimpanzees played happily with the offspring of a local population of baboons. Was it simply because the young primates were too young to have realised the differences between them? Or was it because – as I secretly rather hope – some animals have an inherent appetite for play that overcomes the species barrier? That would certainly explain one of the most delightful occasions I've ever experienced, when on a visit to Arnhem Zoo in the Netherlands I watched a baby gorilla play with a baby orang-utan. Bulkier, heavier and stronger, the gorilla looked like it would win the wrestling match at any moment, but each time it seemed to be on the point of victory, the little orang-utan would stretch out one of its long arms and pull the gorilla's legs from under him. Both apes then collapsed delightedly in a tangled heap.

Within a single species, however, it's easier to see signs of some sort of consciousness and examples of selfless behaviour. Meerkats, the most telegenic of desert mammals, famously combine guard duties and even baby-sit each other's young. Then again, they have to co-operate and stay in a group. A lone meerkat would die very quickly. But one of the most powerful examples was told to me by a game warden who ran a private wildlife park near the Kruger National Park, in South Africa. One particular evening, he was watching a group of elephants drinking at a waterhole when one unusual-looking elephant pushed to the front. It had almost no trunk at all, clearly having lost most of it in a fight or accident, or possibly through infection. Such a disfigured elephant should have died very quickly, but instead the game warden watched in genuine amazement as several elephants – one after the other – used their own healthy trunks to suck up water and then squirted that water into the mouth of the elephant who couldn't drink for herself.

For an animal to show that sort of empathy for another and to follow it up with genuinely altruistic behaviour is nothing short of astonishing. It's certainly enough to make me think that we shouldn't be too quick to explain away the life-saving heroics of Moko, the dolphin. It's this sort of evidence of higher thinking which convinces me that we do have to give animals the benefit of the doubt. It might just be that they're not so dumb after all.

Source: Aubrey Manning, *Daily Mail*, 14th March 2008.

# Do animals have emotions?

A three-month-old baby died in its mother's arms earlier this month. For hours the mother, Gana, gently shook and stroked her son Claudio, apparently trying to restore movement to his lolling head and limp arms. People who watched were moved to tears – unfazed by the fact that Gana and Claudio were 'only' gorillas in Münster zoo, northern Germany. Some, to be fair, reacted differently. One newspaper writer asked bluntly whether we are 'too quick to project human feelings onto animals'. However, Dr Bill Sellers, a primatologist at Manchester University, believes gorillas experience pain and loss in a similar way to humans, 'but of course it's extremely difficult to prove scientifically'.

As Einstein said: 'Not everything that counts can be counted, and not everything that can be counted, counts.' Only a few years ago doctors did not give anaesthetics to tiny babies, believing they did not feel pain. By focusing narrowly on specifics – in this case, the emotional capacity of animals – scientists may fail to take account of what seems obvious and meaningful to the rest of us.

Many of those who commented on Gana's story online took a robustly anti-science line, asking angrily how 'experts' could be so idiotic. 'Have they not heard a cow calling for days when her calves are removed?' asked one. Others described how dogs and cats had become 'depressed' by the death of their own kind – and indeed by the loss of human companions. These people would turn the sceptics' question on its head: 'Haven't we been rather slow to recognise that animals have emotions?'

The question goes to the heart of our way of life. If animals have feelings, it is much harder to justify experimenting on them in laboratories, ogling them in zoos and farming them intensively – or, indeed, at all. The academics attempting to resolve this fall into two camps. Behaviourists accept only the results of tests, rejecting any unproven suggestion that animals think or feel or are even capable of emotion. Ethologists, on the other hand, are prepared to draw conclusions from studies, anecdote and personal observation.

Ethologists, these days, are in the ascendant. One of the best known is Marc Bekoff, professor of biology at the University of Colorado. Sceptical behaviourists often ask him, 'How do you know dogs and elephants feel joy or jealousy or embarrassment?' Bekoff replies: 'One retort is to say: how do you know they don't? Darwin said there was continuity in evolution, so the differences between species are differences in degree rather than differences in kind. They're shades of grey. If we feel jealousy, then dogs and wolves and elephants and chimpanzees feel jealousy. Animal emotions are not necessarily identical to ours but there's no reason to think they should be. Their hearts and stomachs and brains also differ from ours, but this doesn't stop us from saying they have hearts, stomachs and brains. There's dog joy and chimpanzee joy and pig joy, and dog grief, chimpanzee grief and pig grief.'

Many people would feel comfortable associating emotions with large, charismatic mammals, but hard evidence increasingly suggests that other animals are similarly capable. Dr Nathan Emery, a neuropsychologist at Cambridge University's department of zoology, suggests that in their cognitive ability, corvids – the bird family that includes crows, ravens, rooks, jackdaws, jays and magpies – rival the great apes.

Esther Woolfson, author of a new book, *Corvus: A life with birds*, has lived for years with a variety of these 'feathered apes'. Woolfson doesn't believe that her birds understand every word she says – the claim of pet owners everywhere – but she does believe they have emotions. 'I have seen in birds – or believe that I have seen – impatience, frustration, anxiety to impart news, affection, fear, amusement (the last being a difficult one, I admit, to prove, merely based on the look on a magpie's face as its booby-trap was successful) and, particularly, joy.' One bird, Spike, would balance an object – a pamphlet, a rubber glove, a matchbox – on top of a half-open cupboard door, then wait until it fell onto the head of the next person to open the cupboard. Her birds also seemed to empathise: 'To have a magpie, on seeing me weep, hover on top of the fridge, wings outstretched, then fly down to my knee to crouch, squeaking quietly, edging ever nearer until his body was close against mine, seemed to me an act of an unexpected tenderness that I can interpret only as empathy.'

Bekoff agrees that we can no longer associate emotion only with the charismatic mammals: 'The fact is that fish show fear. Rodents can empathise. This is hard science. With birds and mammals there is no doubt that they have a very rich ensemble of emotions.'

Satish Kumar, editor of *Resurgence* magazine, was for several years a Jain monk. The Jain respect for life is extreme: Kumar didn't wash his hair for years in case there were fleas in it. He gave up being a monk eventually, for other reasons, but still believes that all living beings should be respected. 'We are animals. And we have a kind of empathy with the animal kingdom. They're our kin. There is only a slight difference between a cat and a dog and a chimp, and between a female human and a male one, and a black human and a white one. These differences are very small: 98% of our DNA is the same as in animals such as primates,' Kumar says. 'There used to be a time when people thought that animals had no soul, just as they thought that slaves or Africans or women had no soul. We realised a long time ago, as Jains, that animals have souls. They do feel pain and joy. Mostly they feel what we feel. Animals have empathy and intelligence. We have to be humble and accept that we are only one kind of animal and these are others.'

Studies of intelligence and ability have been around for ever – a new one last week showed that elephants can do maths. However, intelligence is not the same as emotion. Evidence of emotional capacity, conceivably older in evolutionary terms than intelligence, has the greater potential to change the way we treat animals. You might put an animal into a circus if it did tricks, but if you knew that this upset the animal you would take it out again. (Unless you were a psychopath, many of whom have been shown to be cruel to animals as well as humans.)

However, even in humans it is difficult to measure emotion. Ultimately, the minds and feelings of individuals other than ourselves are private. 'Access is limited because we can't really get into the head or heart of another being – and that includes other people,' says Bekoff.

Adapted from 'Look deep into her eyes …' by John-Paul Flintoff, *Sunday Times*, 24th August 2008.

# Answers – Unit 28

2   Text 28A: facts and opinions:

Facts:
- volunteers had failed to get the whales to return to deeper water
- the whales moved after Moko appeared
- animals don't usually perform selfless acts
- the explanation is usually one of confused identity because of faulty imprinting
- dolphins have a history of coming to the aid of distressed mammals, including humans
- there are many examples of animal cooperation
- chimpanzees play with baboons in Tanzania/Lake Tanganyika
- gorillas play with orang-utans in zoos
- selfless behaviour among same species is quite common
- meerkats look after each other
- meerkats would not survive if they did not watch out for each other
- elephants help injured members of their group

Opinions:
- this is one of the most amazing cases of inter-species cooperation
- Moko called to the whales
- the whales were saved by the dolphin
- this was a selfless act
- Moko may have mistaken the whales for dolphins
- young animals may not understand the differences between species
- animals like playing so much they don't care if it's with another species
- some animals show evidence of higher thinking / elephants can do maths
- many psychopaths treat both animals and humans cruelly

5   Text 28B: facts and opinions:

Facts:
- a gorilla mother in a zoo stroked her dead baby
- babies used to not be given anaesthetic in the belief they did not feel pain
- there are two types of scientists working with animals, with opposite views
- Jain monks believe that humans should not hurt any living creature
- 98% of human DNA is shared with primates
- intelligence is not the same as emotion
- it is difficult to assess emotional levels even in humans

Opinions:
- we are too quick to project human feelings onto animals
- gorillas experience pain and loss in a similar way to humans
- scientists may not see the obvious
- cows cry when their calves are removed
- dogs can get depressed by the death of a canine or human companion
- we are too slow to recognise that animals have emotions
- if animals have feelings it is hard to justify experimenting on them, putting them in zoos or farming them
- species differ in degree rather than kind
- animals can feel their own kind of joy and grief
- cognitive ability and emotion are also found in birds, fish and rodents
- animals have souls
- we should accept that we are only one animal among many
- we would treat animals differently if we believed they had emotions
- we can never know what another creature is feeling

**Acknowledgements**

The author and publishers are grateful for the permissions granted to reproduce texts in either the original or adapted form. While every effort has been made, it has not always been possible to identify the sources of all the materials used, or to trace all copyright holders. If any omissions are brought to our notice, we will be happy to include the appropriate acknowledgements on reprinting.

Information about the CIE 0500 syllabus in the Introduction is reproduced by permission of the University of Cambridge Local Examinations Syndicate; p. 2 used by permission of Noble Caledonia Ltd; p. 3 advert for Treyn Holidays, used with permission; p. 7 excerpt from 'The Wall' by William Sansom, copyright © William Sansom, 1944; p. 10 'Monty's Method' by Harvey McGavin in the *TES*, September 2001; p. 18 adapted from 'Continental drifters' from *The Sunday Times Magazine* © NI Syndication; p. 19 'Tokyo' by Andrew Miller for British Airways *High Life* magazine, September 2008, reprinted by permission of United Agents Limited on behalf of Andrew Miller; p. 25 excerpt from *Boy* by Roald Dahl © 1984 published by Jonathan Cape Ltd & Puffin Books Ltd, used by permission of David Higham Associates and Farrar, Straus & Giroux LLC; p. 26 excerpt from *My Family and Other Animals* by Gerald Durrell, reproduced with permission of Curtis Brown Group Ltd, London, on behalf of the Estate of Gerald Durrell, copyright © Gerald Durrell 1956; p. 30 'The Pedestrian' by Ray Bradbury reprinted by permission of Don Congdon Associates Inc, © 1951 by the Fortnightly Publishing Company, renewed 1971 by Ray Bradbury; p. 36 excerpt from *Lord of the Flies* by William Golding, published by Faber and Faber Ltd, copyright 1954, renewed © 1982 by William Gerald Golding, used by permission of G.P. Putnam's Sons, a division of Penguin Group (USA) Inc; p. 37 excerpt from *The Woman in Black* by Susan Hill, published by Vintage, © Susan Hill 1983, reproduced by permission of Sheil Land Associates Ltd; p. 43 excerpt from *Rebecca* by Daphne Du Maurier reproduced by permission of Curtis Brown Group Ltd, London on behalf of the Chichester Partnership, copyright © Daphne Du Maurier 1938; p. 46 used by permission of The James H. W. Thompson Foundation, Bangkok; p. 52 'Maid in Japan' by Elizabeth Davies © *The Independent*, 2005; p. 59 adapted from 'Cousteau and his incredible Trojan shark' by Matthew Campbell, *The Sunday Times*, October 2005 © NI Syndication; p. 61 adapted from 'My six nights up a tree' by Barbie Dutter, August 2007 © Telegraph Media Group Limited 2007; p. 74 adapted from 'Relative values: Amaral Samacumbi and his brother, Luis' from *The Sunday Times*, February 2008 © NI Syndication; p. 77 excerpt from *Dear Mrs Parks – A Dialogue with Today's Youth* by permission of Lee & Low Books Inc; p. 81 excerpt from *Native Speaker* by Chang-Rae Lee, copyright © 1995 by Chang-Rae Lee, used by permission of Granta Books and Riverhead Books, an imprint of Penguin Group (USA) Inc; p. 83 adapted from 'My life on hold' by Jane Cassidy © *The Independent* 2005; p. 87 adapted from 'Hello, class, I'm the 16-year-old head' by Dean Nelson, *The Sunday Times*, June 2008 © NI Syndication; p. 90 'A boarder's view' by Donald McGregor, used by permission of the author; p. 97 adapted from 'Fur and against' by AA Gill, *The Sunday Times*, December 2008 © NI Syndication; p. 99 used by permission of PETA; p. 104 adapted from 'Stoopid: why the Google generation isn't as smart as it thinks' by Bryan Appleyard, *The Sunday Times*, July 2008 © NI Syndication; p. 107 adapted from 'Office staff hit delete in war on e-mail monster' by John Harlow, *The Sunday Times*, October 2007 © NI Syndication; p. 121 excerpt from *Touching the Void* by Joe Simpson published by Jonathan Cape, reprinted by permission of The Random House Group Ltd and HarperCollins Publishers, copyright © 1989 by Joe Simpson; pp. 128–9 'The Fairly Intelligent Fly' from *Fables for Our Time & Famous Poems Illustrated* by James Thurber © 1940 by Rosemary A. Thurber, 'The Peacelike Mongoose' and 'The Bears and the Monkeys' from *Further Fables for Our Time* by James Thurber © 1956 by Rosemary A. Thurber: reprinted by arrangement with Rosemary A. Thurber and The Barbara Hogenson Agency, Inc, all rights reserved; p. 137 adapted from 'Mike Hollingshead, storm chaser' from *The Sunday Times*, October 2007 © NI Syndication; p. 146 adapted from 'The kiddie killing fields' by India Knight, *The Sunday Times*, February 2005 © NI Syndication; p. 149 'There will come soft rains' from *The Martian Chronicles* by Ray Bradbury, reprinted by permission of Don Congdon Associates Inc; p. 158 adapted from 'Well done class, you learnt zilch' by Chris Woodhead, *The Sunday Times*, April 2007 © NI Syndication; p. 161 adapted from 'Animal magic' by Aubrey Manning, the Daily Mail; p. 163 adapted from 'Look deep into her eyes...' by John-Paul Flintoff, *The Sunday Times*, August 2008 © NI Syndication.

Thanks to the following for permission to reproduce photographs and images:
(**Key:** *t* = top, *b* = bottom, *c* = centre, *l* = left, *r* = right)
p. 2 Noble Caledonia Ltd; p. 10 Image courtesy of Monty and Pat Roberts Inc, photo by Christopher Dyke; p. 19 Tokyo illustration by Tobias Hickey; p. 116*t* Bollywood Tents; pp. 116*b*, 135 Marian Cox; p. 117*tr* 'zeroHouse' by Sprecht Harpman Architects © 2009; p. 117*tl* 'One family house in Rohrdorf/Germany (Black Forest)' by Kauffmann Theilig & Partner, Freie Architekten BDA, Stuttgart/Germany, photograph by Roland Halbe Architekturfotografie, Stuttgart/Germany; p. 117*tcr* Jan Oliehoek; p. 117*cl* John Glenn & Co Photography; pp. 117*bcr*, 118*tr* Michael Jantzen; p. 117*br* Gail Johnson/Alamy; p. 117*bl* Michael Dwyer/Alamy; p. 118*tl* Arco Images GmbH/Alamy; p. 118*cl* David Noble Photography/Alamy; p. 118*bl* H. Mark Weidman Photography/Alamy; p. 118*br* Martin Garnham/Alamy; p. 127 Ivy Close Images/Alamy; p. 137 Mike Hollingshead; p. 139 Lisa Eastman/Alamy; p. 150 I. Glory/Alamy; p. 153*tr* Wikimedia Commons; p. 153*cr* 'L.H.O.O.Q. Mona Lisa with moustache', 1930 (colour litho), Duchamp, Marcel (1887–1968)/Private Collection/© DACS/Cameraphoto Arte Venezia/The Bridgeman Art Library, © Succession Marcel Duchamp/Man Ray Trust/ADAGP, Paris and DACS, London 2010; p. 153*br* Udronotto aka Marco Pece; p. 153*bl* David Parry/PA Archive/Press Association Images; p. 154*tr* Rui Vieira/PA Archive/Press Association Images; p. 154*tl* Stan Kujawa/Alamy; p. 154*bl* Time & Life Pictures/Getty Images.